MW01600228

Endorsements

"Ciara has a unique ability to take seemingly complicated topics and make them simple to understand while also keeping your attention.

By reading this book you're sure to be able to tap into and use your intuition to improve your life. Ciara's vulnerability has a powerful way of showing you what's possible as she gives you the simple steps to tap into your own intuition."

-**Krissy Chin,**
podcast host and author of Sell While You Sleep

"Interactive, solution-focused, and endearingly cheeky, "You Always Know" is the extremely comprehensive guiding light we all need to dust off our third eye chakras and move into an intuition-led life. Ciara Rubin has cultivated a brilliant catalyst for the Age of Light paradigm we are all moving into.

Through "You Always Know," Ciara has thoughtfully transcribed the often abstract worlds of clairvoyance and beyond into a relatable and down-to-earth masterpiece. I highly recommend "You Always Know" to anyone who is looking to transform their relationship with their intuition, no matter if you are a curious beginner or a woo-woo veteran: powerful insights, activities, and an overall fun time are all contained in this book."

-Savannah Rose Johnson,
author of Ghosts & Letters and CEO of Eclipse Evolution

"Author Ciara Rubin is vulnerable, candid, playful, yet brutally honest, in providing a down and dirty way to help you dive DEEP into yourself.

You Always Know took me on a journey into my own shadows and gave me clear exercises to help me heal and learn to trust myself. I learned I am deeply clairsentient, and because of this book I've learned to trust what I'm feeling in my body with confidence. This book is a goldmine no matter if you're new to intuition development, or an old pro."

-Jessica Anderson,
Author of My Body Says and My Body: I Say Yes or No

"Ciara is a charismatic, eloquent, and fierce mystic whose words linger with the wisdom of all ages boiled down into simple and straightforward advice and insight. This book is nothing short of a timeless how to on how to be the best you!"

-Masha Loddy,
Shadow Work & Plant Medicine Integration Guide

You Always Know:

4 Step Guide for Empaths to Stop Second
Guessing and Trust Your Intuition

By
Ciara Rubin

I dedicate this book to my beautiful children.
Without you I wouldn't know all I'm capable of
or how much love is possible in one life.
Thank you my darlings!

Table of Contents

Introduction

I can promise you I will always be raw and honest with you. To reveal the darkest parts of myself and also shine the brightest parts. To show you what's possible when you develop your intuition and have the courage to trust it. I hope that the hard evidence of my life will inspire you to come on this journey with me.

All I can teach you is from my own experience. I'm not a doctor of psychology. I'm not a fourth-generation psychic. I'm just a girl, an empath, who had the balls to dig deeper. To look beyond the mundane material world. I've always had a sense that there's much more to this world and the human experience than meets the eye. I know you have that same sense.

I spent the first part of my life preparing to live a dream that wasn't mine. It was a good dream, I guess. At least, a celebrated dream. I was going to light up the stages of New York and then the world. I've been singing since age 10. My parents supported my desire to become a famous Broadway performer.

Then, I did the next acceptable thing: go to college and get my degree. Halfway through my time there, I realized the truth. That this wasn't my dream. I was living to fulfill the unfulfilled desires and aspirations of those around me. I was searching for the external validation of fame instead of doing my art for art's sake. This was a crushing realization.

I finally told my parents during my senior year, and their disappointment was worse. The silence on the other end of the phone cried, "But you're so talented!" As I shook the expectations, I knew I was free, yet I felt completely lost.

If I wasn't going to become the Performing Artist as designated on my bachelor's degree, what was I going to do? If I only liked to sing and perform as a hobby, who was I meant to be in the world? I had no fucking idea.

I definitely didn't trust that I knew the answers. I've made all the wrong decisions. I spent thousands of dollars on an education that I probably wasn't going to use. I worked in the service industry as a waitress and bartender. I definitely drank too much. I was fresh from a self-destructive relationship with a binge alcoholic.

Finally, I broke up with the alcoholic and started dating a sweet, intelligent guy. Once my boyfriend proposed, I knew it was time to grow up and do something more with my life. I accepted a job as Director of Operations for my local chamber of commerce. I embraced the skirt suits, shaking hands with the mayor on the reg and all the other perks that came along with the job.

I was planning large-scale events and getting my feet wet with public speaking. Yet, I still felt almost dead inside. Like, why isn't this good enough? I'm doing something that makes everyone in my life super proud of me. I always get free hair blow-outs, free appetizers, and the like. Why doesn't it feel as good as I thought it would? Something about it felt fake, like a thin veneer of silly self-importance.

It's such a contrast to where I am now. I'm married to my lover and best friend. We're building businesses and raising our two beautiful children together. I've got two empowered home births under my belt. I spend my free time teaching spirituality, singing in a local rock band, and traveling. Trusting my intuition is what got me here.

My deep satisfaction in knowing who I really am is something that no one can ever take away from me. This is exactly what I want for you:

- To strip away all the conditioning of society and other people's dreams.

- To shine a light deep inside your soul. To discover (perhaps with surprise) that you might actually like what you see.

- To change or embrace all the things you don't like about yourself.

- To remember ALL of who you are, even the dark parts.

- To see the truth of the beauty and the power that lives inside you.

Your intuition is the path into that world. Into that version of yourself. At least it was for me. As an empath, it's always crucial to feel my way through this process. I invite you to do the same. Ask yourself, how does this feel? If it feels exciting and/ or a little outside your comfort zone, you're on the right track.

The first thing to understand when developing your intuition is intuition itself. What is intuition? What is the experience of your intuition like? How does intuitive information come to you? There are four main intuitive senses. I'll help you figure out which senses are your primary and secondary. This is what we'll dive into in Step One.

In Step Two, things are going to get intense in the best way possible. We're going to be diving deep into your darkness, facing your demons together. This is Shadow Work. Shadow Work is the biggest missing piece in most modern intuition development. You have to take a look at your fears, heal from past pain, and be willing to set yourself free. Otherwise, your intuition will always be shrouded in darkness. So, in Step Two, we'll walk together as I share:

- What shadows actually are

- How shadows prevent you from trusting your intuition

- How shadows block you from manifesting the life you desire

- How to heal your shadows in 7 steps.

Then it gets fun as we explore dream work together. Every night, you're having dreams, whether or not you're aware of them. I bet you had some super vivid dreams when you were a kid! It's time to bring that natural ability back into the forefront of your awareness. Your dreams are full of clues about exactly why you're struggling.

They shine a light on the areas of your life that you find stressful. Dreams are full of examples of what you need to do to clear your blocks and trust yourself and your intuition. I'll teach you how to tap into the practical magic of your dreams.

Once you are well aware of your fears, shadows, and dysfunctional behaviors, you're going to need a strong spiritual self-care practice. It gets weird: energy vampires, daily life overwhelms, and difficult relationships. Spiritual self-care is the key to taking on your day with energy and passion to feeling safe in this scary world.

As an empath, you're hella sensitive. In the past, you may have seen that sensitivity as a drawback or handicap, but it's actually a superpower. This is what we'll dive into in Step Three.

After you:

- Know how your intuitive information comes in
- Are clearing your shadows
- Properly care for your energy

You're going to be experiencing your intuition on a level you never have before. Intuitive nudges, signs, and downloads are going to be coming at you from everywhere. You need to understand exactly **what** your intuition is telling you and have proof that the messages are real. This is part of what we will cover in Step 4.

Finally, I'm going to introduce you to the super fun and moving practice of intuitive Tarot. Forget all you've heard about the Tarot being evil or difficult to learn. You'll be able to read and interpret the messages your intuition is sending you. Then, you'll turn those messages into practical action steps.

What I'm going to teach you in this book is a holistic way to develop your intuition to the point of trusting it. I won't give you some "little exercises" to develop each of your Clairs. This 4-step system is an entire spiritual path in itself.

Many spiritual paths will interest you, and I encourage you to follow your curiosity! This is the age of sovereign spirituality. AKA: you take bits and pieces of the paths and disciplines that resonate with you and leave the rest.

Don't make any one spiritual path a religion because that's when the message starts to get muddled. Spirituality then becomes less about enlightenment and more about control. The message is more important than the messenger. I hope the messages in this book help you empower yourself and love yourself.

Remember and fall in love with the truth that you are so much more than your five senses. That your intuition is simply a deeper expression of your human experience. I hope that as you follow the steps laid out in each chapter, you begin or continue to remember all of who and what you are.

That's what this book is going to help you do:

- Learn the languages of your intuition
- Develop your intuition to the point where you completely trust it
- Live making decisions from that place

Besides my personal stories and the key learning points associated with those stories, there are:

- Fun quizzes
- Simple exercises
- Quick practices

Complete these exercises in your journal or in the You Always Know Workbook. If you don't have the workbook yet, you can find it at https://ciararubin.com/yakbookresources/

The choice is yours:

1. Stay where you are and keep living a life that's killing your true self

2. Accept the challenge and choose to step into everything that is possible for you

It sounds intense, and it is. I don't say it lightly because I'm living it. If I hadn't done the things outlined in this book, I would have stayed an angry, gossipy, hard-edged girl with no idea why things were never working out the way I wanted.

Now that my tough love rant is over… Take it one step at a time. If each chapter takes you about a week to get through, that would be ideal, but if it takes longer, no worries. Honor your energy (and don't use honoring your energy as an excuse- been there!). And hey, you could zip through each Step in a few days. I don't underestimate you, Queen!

As you dive into this story, I hope you see yourself in it. That you are not alone in your struggles. As dark as things have ever been for you, they have been for me, too.

I hope you know that you are not broken. You're covered by layers of armor you've used to protect yourself, to survive your upbringing and a fear-filled world. I'll help you shed that armor in the knowing that what is underneath is much more powerful than you realize. That it is safe, finally, for you to be powerful and also loved. I hope you can live knowing that your magic is needed. That magic is real. And that you, yes, YOU, are psychic. I love you today and every day! Now, take my hand, and let's begin.

STEP 1:
Clair Awakening

Chapter 1:
I Fell to My Knees

I fell to my knees in the shower and prayed for the first time in my life. It was January 2015, and the impending Ebola crisis was scaring me out of my skin. You know, that disease that eats your flesh? We were on the brink of a possible global pandemic, and I'd returned home from a major "prepping" grocery shop. My arms were laden with bags of flour, dried beans, oils, vitamins, and other medical supplies.

Needless to say, I was having an absolute panic attack. I put the groceries away and stepped into the shower. The shower has been my place of refuge since childhood, so I let the water drown my sorrows. But the panic continued. What if everyone I loved died? What if everyone around me died? What if I got Ebola? What if the entire infrastructure of the world fell?

For most of my life, I'd had no real spiritual beliefs. I'd never had a true experience with any "God" or "Spirit" that I remembered. Growing up, my parents let me go to church with friends whenever I wanted to and never pushed religion onto me. Some churches were fun and welcoming. Many were full of hypocrisy and meaningless rituals, as opposed to actual truth.

As I shampooed, I started to cry. As I rinsed, I was sobbing. Before I could put the conditioner into my hair, I fell to my knees, overcome with fear. For the first time in my life, I called out, "God?!" to no one. To my utter surprise, I felt tingles all over my body. I called out again, "is someone there?!" Again, I felt full body pins and needles and a huge YES. I decided I'd play along. So I asked, "what should I call you?" And in my head, I heard the word "GOD," clear as crystal.

This shocked me because I have a lot of baggage around the word "god." Considering my background with religion, feeling ostracized by most religious people I'd ever met, being told I needed to be "saved" while they talked shit about me behind my back... when I heard this nothingness, this presence, say the word "God," I was more than a little surprised.

But in my state of fear, the spiritual experience and truth I was feeling in my body entranced me. So again, I played along and said, "Please, God, do not let this Ebola outbreak happen. I promise that if you don't let this happen, I will do what I came here to do. I will let you work through me, and my life purpose will belong to you."

Once more, I felt the sensation, and as it left, I felt massive relief. Now that I was getting used to it, I noticed it felt warm and satisfying. One month later, I had my first-ever Psychic reading.

When my new friend, Ally, invited me to the Psychic Fair, I was intrigued and excited to have a pretty & smart new friend.

I didn't realize those kinds of things existed in the Southeast! It definitely seemed more common in California, where I was born.

My heart was racing as I signed up for two tarot readings. As we sat down to wait for our turn, we passed a woman doing Aura readings. If you don't know, your aura is the energy body around your physical body.

She looked up at me from her chair and asserted, "You're an empath, aren't you?!" My Mom had always talked about the women in our family being empaths. All I knew was that it meant I could read someone's energy. Even if they told me one thing, I knew the truth about what was going on with them. Obviously, I immediately signed up for a reading with her.

I don't remember what the other two readers said at all. When I sat across from the aura reader, she asked me if I'd ever had any weird or "paranormal" experiences. Immediately, an experience that I hadn't thought about in over a decade popped into my mind.

I was 13 years old and had recently moved to Georgia from California. One of my favorite things about life in California was Girl Scouts (I did it for 8 years!), so I joined a new Troop when I moved. It was a nice transition to help me cope with the culture shock. The experience happened at a sleepover birthday party for one of the girls in the Troop.

After we snuggled into our sleeping bags, staying awake and talking about 13-year-old girl things, I'm pretty sure I suggested doing a seance. I don't remember if it was me who suggested it, but I can only assume, considering what happened next. We lit a few candles, sat in a circle, and held hands. I stated loud and clear that any spirits who were good spirits were welcome to come into this space to communicate any messages they had for us.

Almost immediately, images started flooding my mind. I thought I was making it up, so all in good fun, I started to say the things I was seeing in my head out loud. I spoke of a sweet but stern old man, about six foot two, with a slight hunch in his back. He was wearing blue jeans, a T-shirt, a zippered hoodie, and playing pool. He told me that he was a pool shark and gave me an old man wink from his glittering eyes and toothbrush mustache face.

As I continued to give specific details of what I was seeing in my mind's eye, the birthday girl gasped. She said, "I wasn't sure where you were going with this, but when you said he called himself a pool shark, I knew. It's my grandfather! He died."

She then proceeded to break down and cry. On her birthday! I made the birthday girl cry on her birthday! I felt terrible, yet I also felt absolute awe that the messages I was bringing through were real. I thought I was making it up and having some fun. Turns out I was doing some legit mediumship.

When I finished telling the aura reader the story, she gave me a tiny, knowing smile. "You can do what I can do," she said matter-of-factly. "You're psychic. I can feel that you're meant to be a teacher of spirituality, a leader. Have you ever considered getting some tarot cards?"

Stunned, I thought, *Lady, are you crazy? I'm finally doing everything right. I've got a big girl job with lots of perks. I married an amazing man that my parents approved of, and we bought our first house. What in the actual hell?!* Underneath all that logic was a tiny voice that I had never listened to, and it said, "YES." I felt the tingles in my body that I'd felt that day in the shower.

Well, I'd asked for it. I told a so-called God that I'd let it work through me and do whatever it wanted me to do. No Ebola pandemic had come to pass, thank goodness. And now here I was, being called into so-called leadership in a field I knew nothing about. I mean, I'd always been into astrology and identified as an empath. My Aunt teaches Tantra, but I always thought that was just about Sexual Healing (LOL)! But a promise is a promise, and I always keep my promises. So I decided to trust that tiny voice, and after I left that day, I ordered my first deck of Angel Tarot cards.

Intuitive abilities are not limited to a special few people. Intuition and psychic abilities are simply an untapped part of the human experience. It's crucial that you understand that you are as intuitive as any other person. That you are psychic. You don't need to be a "third-generation witch." You don't need to have had powerful abilities and experiences since you were a child. You don't even need to have had a near-death experience.

You are as psychic as the most psychic person out there. Being intuitive is like having another set of muscles. All you have to do to make them strong is give them some attention and flex them on the reg.

The first thing I had to learn is the first thing I'll teach you here. If you're going to trust that tiny voice inside, you need to get to know it and all the ways it communicates with you. That tiny voice is your intuition. The Clairs are the languages of your intuition. The Clairs are your four main intuitive senses.

Chapter 2:
Clairsentience

How it Works

Clairsentience means clear feeling. This is the Intuitive sense most linked to the empath. Clairsentience indicates a clear sense of emotions and physical sensations in the body.

This intuitive sense is located in four different energy centers or chakras within the body: the solar plexus, the heart chakra, and, by extension, the two hand chakras. The hands are an extension of the heart chakra because when you're in the womb, your hands grow out of your heart space.

See diagram.

The chakras correlate with the spectrum of visible light, which is why they're the colors of the rainbow. Starting at the root chakra with the color red, all the way up to the crown chakra with the color violet.

See diagram.

For clairsentience, the solar plexus chakra resonates with the color yellow, and the heart/hand chakras resonate with the color green.

The chakras associated with Clairsentience are deep within the body, so you can feel Clairsentience in your body. This could be subtle sensations in your gut or solar plexus. It could be a heartache or an opening sensation in your chest. You can even feel subtle sensations and energies with your hands.

Experiencing Clairsentience

Now that you're more familiar with Clairsentience, let's talk about what the experience of receiving Clairsentient information is actually like.

Gut Feelings

This experience is one I'm sure you can identify with. You may get a gut feeling that something isn't right. Even if everything seems fine and everyone else seems fine with it. You're able to see through the veil of other people's defense mechanisms and the lies they're telling themselves. For example, you may ask someone how they're doing, and they say good, but you can tell they're anxious.

You might get a gut feeling for something that feels like the next level of empowerment and/or happiness. It may not be logical or go along with what your family or mainstream society would find acceptable. For example, I had a gut feeling about the birth of my babies being unmedicated and outside of the hospital system. Almost everyone I knew thought I was crazy, but I listened to my gut and succeeded!

As a clairsentient, your gut feelings are your compass. If you're brave enough to listen, they'll lead you to places of ultimate magic and deep satisfaction.

Sympathy Pains

A sympathy pain is a low-level or matched-intensity pain that isn't connected to dysfunction in your body. It's connected to dysfunction in someone else's body. This will happen especially with someone you love or care about.

For example, you may feel a pain in your shoulder if someone you love has had shoulder surgery. You might feel an ache in your heart and then later find out that one of your best friends has experienced some type of heartbreak or emotional pain. Sympathy pains are not limited to physical injury.

You may even experience a sympathy pain prophecy, where you feel pain in an area where a loved one has a disorder or dysfunction they don't know about yet. You might feel annoyed with this ability, yet it's useful, especially if you want to be a healer of some kind. If you're bothered by your sympathy pain ability, you can give it less attention, and it will start to fade.

Phantom Sensations

Phantom sensations may sound like sympathy pains, but there is a distinction. You will never feel any actual pain with a phantom sensation. You may feel as though someone is gently putting a hand on a part of your body. You may feel a tingling sensation, and you may even feel a change in temperature in either part or your entire body.

You could interpret phantom sensations as faded sympathy pains. Yet, in my experience, phantom sensations are less linked to connecting with other people's energy and more linked to your higher self, letting you know what's happening within your body.

Anxiety

Most clairsentients experience a moderate to extreme amount of anxiety in their life. The anxiety may come and go in waves during stressful periods of your life. Yet, it's an experience that always seems to crop up.

The biggest reason empaths experience anxiety is due to their sensitivity. They're able to sense the anxieties and fears of the people around them. People in crowds, and even the anxiety and fear of the human collective here on Earth. Because of this, empaths often have difficulty distinguishing what anxiety is theirs and what anxiety isn't theirs. This is why it is crucial to practice spiritual self-care, which we will cover in Step 3.

Anxiety often makes many empaths feel like they are victims of their circumstances. Like their sensitivity is a hindrance. This couldn't be further from the truth. Your sensitivity is your superpower. It's your ability to sense your truth and the truth of others so that you can navigate the world in a way that's real. Your sensitivity is even more valuable if you feel called to use your empathic abilities to help others.

Are you a Primary Clairsentient?

Now that you understand the experience of clairsentience, here are four qualifying traits. These will help you determine if clairsentience is your primary intuitive sense.

Highly Sensitive Person (HSP)

This is one of the buzz phrases used to describe someone who is primarily clairsentient. It's become popular in the past decade or so. According to hsperson.com, an HSP is someone who is easily overwhelmed by intense sensations like loud sounds, bright lights, and/or strong smells. This is someone who gets rattled when they have a lot to do in a short amount of time. An HSP has a rich and complex inner life and may have been called either "too sensitive or shy" as a child.

Empath

I've mentioned this word a lot when talking about clairsentience. In my definition, an empath is someone who's sensitive and attuned to feelings. An empath is also someone who's more sensitive than others to certain substances, like medication, alcohol, or caffeine. Empaths tend to have a childlike innocence hidden underneath either a tough exterior or shyness. They're excellent friends and parents.

People Pleaser

If you're primarily clairsentient, you may be a recovering or still struggling people-pleaser. Clairsentients usually have a hard time saying no, especially when someone needs help. They can often get into relationships with people who are serial takers, energy vampires, and narcissists. Many clairsentients struggle with a fear of being alone or abandoned and often betray themselves for love.

Obvi, this is not healthy and will be part of our discussion in the chapters on spiritual self-care. I'll give you some tools to heal and maintain healthy, reciprocal relationships. Know that if you struggle with any of the above, you're most definitely clairsentient.

Digestion Issues

As mentioned above, clairsentience is centered in the heart and solar plexus chakras. Located in your gut, the solar plexus chakra is linked to confidence and your personal power. Often, people who are primarily clairsentient struggle to feel confident being all of who they are. Physically, this manifests as digestion issues. This can range from food sensitivities and gas to leaky gut syndrome and even moderate or severe IBS. Many empaths struggle with food addictions to sugar, alcohol, fried foods, and caffeine.

Important: Don't get caught up in the idea that because you're an empath, you are more likely to have diseases or diagnoses. Empaths are not "more susceptible" to health problems.

Clairsentience Quiz

Take this quiz to discover if Clairsentience is your primary intuitive sense. After taking all four quizzes, compare your results to determine which Clair is your primary and which is your secondary.

If yes, put a 3. If sometimes, put a 2. If no, put a 1 in the box.

You're more sensitive than most to certain foods, substances, and experiences (like horror movies, big crowds, etc.).

You often get gut feelings about people & situations, even if you don't listen to them.

You struggle to say no to people, especially when they're asking for help.

Anxiety is the bane of your existence.

You resonate with the terms "highly sensitive person" and/or "empath."

Clairsentient Experience

Write 3-4 sentences in your journal or workbook about a time when you had a gut feeling about something or someone. What happened?

How to Activate Your Clairsentience

Physical Organs

You need to know which physical organs are associated with your clairsentience. This is an easy way to figure out what's blocking the full activation of your intuition. Any issues in these organs will point to energetic dysfunction within the chakras (solar plexus and heart) connected to it.

I am not a medical doctor and do not claim to know how to heal these organs, body parts, or physical issues.

The physical organs and body parts linked to Clairsentience are:

Solar Plexus Chakra:

- Stomach
- Intestines
- Liver
- Pancreas
- Gallbladder
- Diaphragm
- Kidneys

Heart Chakra:

- Heart
- Lungs
- Thymus
- Arms

- Hands
- Fingers

Physical Issues

When you look at the above list of organs and body parts, do you have any issues or conditions within them? Things like:

Solar Plexus Chakra

- IBS
- Bloating, gas
- Food sensitivities or allergies
- Leaky Gut
- Candida (yeast overgrowth)
- Hyper or Hypoglycemia
- Ulcers in the digestive system
- Liver dysfunction
- Spleen dysfunction
- Pancreas or Gallbladder dysfunction
- Diabetes

Heart Chakra

- Heart issues
- Heart attacks
- Bronchitis
- Asthma

- Allergies
- Breast issues (lumps, cancer)
- Shoulder issues
- Arm or hand issues
- Carpal tunnel syndrome
- Poor posture

Energetic Issues

IMPORTANT: When you're first looking at yourself in this way, it can be a little overwhelming. Stay calm, take a deep breath. You can address these issues one at a time to heal and activate your Clairs.

These are the issues connected to dysfunction in the solar plexus and heart chakras:

Solar Plexus Chakra

- Low self-esteem or self-worth
- Lack of self-confidence
- Indecisiveness
- Poor sense of self
- People pleasing
- Unexpressed anger
- Resentment (of yourself or others)
- Jealousy (in any relationship or situation)
- Self-shame

- Self-loathing
- Guilt
- Comparison to others (in a way that disempowers you)

Write your responses in your journal or workbook.

1. Which solar plexus issue hits deep?

2. Why do you think you struggle with this?

3. How can you change this?

Extra Credit: Answer questions 2 and 3 for each energetic issue listed.

Heart Chakra

- Emotional abuse, neglect, abandonment, or aggression
- Heartbreak (partner, family member, friend)
- Self-betrayal or betrayal by others
- Being ignored
- Feeling like no one truly loves or understands you
- Needing constant reassurance or external emotional validation
- Codependency
- Difficulty trusting others
- Inability to fully fall in love with a partner
- Challenges allowing yourself to be loved
- Difficulty forgiving others who've wronged you
- Difficulty forgiving yourself
- Ghosting people

Write your responses in your journal or workbook.

1. Which energetic heart issue hits deep?

2. Why do you think you struggle with this?

3. How can you change this?

Extra Credit: Answer questions 2 and 3 for each energetic issue listed.

Heal Your Solar Plexus Chakra

Here are some tips on how to heal your solar plexus chakra:

- Tap into and fire up your free will.

You always know what you want to experience. If you have trouble making a decision, it's usually because you're afraid of what someone else will think, say, or do. You KNOW what you want and have the free will to make that decision!

- Figure out and commit to a diet that reflects your ideal lifestyle and what works best for your body.

So much of the food in our modern industrialized world is not actually food but "food product." Eat simple foods. Do your own research to discover what types of foods best honor your unique body and can help eliminate any of the health issues you may be having. Food is medicine, so make sure it's the healthy kind!

- Meditation (I'll give you tips on this in Step 3)

Don't worry, you don't have to sit in silence. You just need to close your eyes and focus on your solar plexus (the space just above your belly button) to clear and power it up!

For a Solar Plexus Chakra Clear, Heal, & Power Up Guided Meditation, visit www.ciararubin.com/yakbookresources

- Exercise (that you enjoy! It doesn't have to be intense cardio)

Move your dang body, girl! Walk, run, dance, lift weights, swim, whatever makes you excited and gives you joy. Make it stupid easy and start with just 5 minutes per day.

- Develop a nightly bedtime routine that helps you wind down at least 1-2 hours before you want to be asleep.

Sleep is everything. Do everything in your power to protect and honor your sleep. Take the freaking TV out of your bedroom.

- Mirror work and affirmations (married with Shadow Work, which I'll cover in Step 2)

This shit is so powerful. Staring into your own eyes? Whew!

For a Guided Mirror Work Experience, visit visit www. ciararubin.com/yakbookresources

- OWN YOUR POWER

You have so much power within you. I know you can feel it. Let your energy shine out; no more taking on the feelings of others. It is safe for you to be powerful!

- Channel your anger into something creative and productive

You can make art. You can throw rocks. You can clean the shit out of your house. Ooo, rage therapy is amazing.

For a Guided Rage Therapy Experience, visit www.ciara-rubin.com/yakbookresources

- Setting healthy boundaries and doing what's best for you

We'll cover this more in Step 3, but just know that that boundary-setting life is coming for you. ;)

- Develop a healthy self-care routine

Self-care is not selfish! We'll dive more into specifics in Step 3.

- Heal how you feel about any relationships with men in your life. The ones who let you down, hurt you, or aren't fulfilling their potential and modeling that for you.

This is a BIG can of worms.

For the "Speaking to the Father" Guided Meditation and the "Forgive that A-Hole" Guided "Ex" Meditation, visit www.ciararubin.com/yakbookresources

- Color Therapy
  - Wear or keep the color yellow around you.
  - Create art with the color yellow.

There's a freaking awesome table containing all of the above information on Activating your Clairsentience in an easy-to-read format; at the end of the book.

Heal Your Heart Chakra

Here are some tips on how to heal your heart chakra:

- Meditation (focused on your heart)

For a Heart Chakra Clear, Heal, & Power Up Guided Meditation, visit www.ciararubin.com/yakbookresources

- Journaling

Get all your grief, anger, and frustration out of your body and onto the paper.

- Expressing your love to loved ones, family members, friends, and pets.

Let them know you love them! Bonus points if you can speak/act out their love language. Is it physical touch? Hug it out. Quality time? Make a date. Words of affirmation? Write them a lovey note. Acts of Service? Make them dinner. Gifts? Think about who they are and what they like.

- Allow yourself to receive love from others.

Make it clear to your loved ones what your main love languages are, and stay open. Watch for examples of them loving you with their love language as well.

- Receive compliments with grace.

When someone compliments you, just say THANK YOU. Don't tell them how XYZ sucks or compliment them back (until you're genuinely inspired to do so). Just bask in the compliment.

- Do things that you love, just for fun!

Let's separate your self-esteem from productivity. Find a hobby or do an activity that you enjoy without needing to "move the ball forward." Watching TV doesn't count!

- Set the intention to journey toward unconditional love and self-love.

A tall order but definitely one of the main points of your human existence. This can begin with radical or unconditional self-acceptance.

- Choose to see that everything serves your highest good, even if it doesn't make logical sense.

You live in a supportive Universe. A Universe that wants the best for you and wants to give you what you want (if it's in your best interest). When challenging things happen, discipline yourself to wait and see how this situation ultimately serves your highest good. I promise you'll be amazed at the results.

- Self-forgiveness

Yes, you. The hardest person to forgive.

For a Self-Forgiveness Guided Meditation, visit www. ciararubin.com/yakbookresources

- Self-compassion

Does beating yourself up really work? Does it actually make you do the thing or stop you from doing the thing? Nope. Take a deep breath and tell yourself it's okay to make mistakes. It's okay to have issues that need healing. You are a GOOD person.

- Develop self-appreciation and self-loving practices and habits.

Eating healthy. Non-toxic body, bath, and house products. GO OUTSIDE.

- Mirror Work

For a Guided Mirror Work Experience, visit www.ciara-rubin.com/yakbookresources

- Forgiving others

Yikes. I'll help you out with this one in Step 2.

- Heal how you feel about any relationships with women in your life. The ones who let you down, hurt you, or aren't fulfilling their potential and modeling that for you.

For the "Speaking to the Mother" Guided Meditation and the "Forgive that B*tch" Guided Meditation, visit www. ciararubin.com/yakbookresources

- Color Therapy

  - Wear or keep the color green around you.

  - Create art with the color green.

REMINDER: There's a freaking awesome table containing all of the above information on Activating your Clairsentience in an easy-to-read format; at the end of the book.

A Note on Clairsentience

Clairsentience is the most powerful intuitive sense for two reasons:

Clairsentience is the only sense centered in TWO of the main chakras: the heart and solar plexus.

Located deep in the body, this sense and its chakras enable you to FEEL the intuitive impulses. You feel these impulses manifest as physical sensations that can throughout your body. I'll elaborate on what these feelings are like in the next few sections.

When you feel something, you know it's true, right? Why is this? It's because the body is in the present moment at all times. Have you heard the spiritual saying that "the present is all we have?" or "Now is all there is?" This is true. Your mind can be lamenting the past or worrying about the future, but your body has no choice but to be in the present. In the now.

Anything you feel in your body is an absolute truth you can trust.

Chapter 3:
Clairvoyance

How it Works

Clairvoyance means "clear seeing." It's the intuitive ability most associated with the psychic. Clairvoyance centers in the third eye chakra, right in the middle of your forehead. The third eye chakra resonates with the color indigo.

See diagram.

Clairvoyant information comes through both your physical eyes and your inner eye. You'll see images, scenes, and visions inside your head (whether your physical eyes are open or closed). You'll also see things with your physical eyes.

Let's talk about the experience of receiving intuitive information via clairvoyance.

Experiencing Clairvoyance

Imagination

Your imagination, otherwise known as the pictures and images you see in your head or your mind's eye, is actually a function of your Clairvoyance. It's always so silly to me when people say, "Oh, it was just your imagination!" Well, yes, it was your imagination, but it wasn't "**just** your imagination." The things you see in your mind's eye could be literal or symbolic. With clairvoyance, they can be both or either one.

When exploring and developing your clairvoyance, it's important to use discernment. Don't take every vision, dream, or picture in your mind as literal. Mastering Clairvoyance requires you to search for the deeper meaning of your imagination. Like a tiny detective!

You may be imagining horrible things or wonderful things, and both have a place in where you are right now. The amount of fear within you will determine the amount of negative thoughts and images. The beautiful daydreams you have will only increase the more you go through this 4 step process. In fact, beautiful daydreams are a discipline that is well worth making a habit.

Dreams

Dreams are most definitely a function of your clairvoyance! You dream every night, whether you remember it or not. Dreams are your soul or the facet of your soul living a life as you right now, exploring the astral realms. If you had vivid dreams as a child, you're definitely Clairvoyant. We're going to dive much deeper into dreams and dream work in Step 2, so stay tuned for that! For now, know that all clairvoyants dream vividly, sometimes lucidly, and they can even have prophetic dreams.

Visual Signs

When it comes to signs from Spirit, you will see and notice them everywhere. This is especially true once you start putting intention and awareness into it. It could be:

- Animals
- Bugs
- Birds
- Feathers
- Lucky pennies
- Things you see on billboards
- Repeating number sequences (angel numbers)

To name a few, they're all around you, and you notice them. These signs can be for encouragement or to give you a specific message.

Clairvoyance is one of the most beautiful and comforting intuitive senses. You can see that God, your angels, and/or your Spirit guides are always around you.

Lights, Shadows, and Apparitions

This may have only happened to you as a child, and it may still happen from time to time. If you're Clairvoyant, you'll see sparkles of light, blinking orbs of light, shadows, shadow people, and even ghosts. You may have shut down this ability in childhood. This often happens because of fear or adults dismissing your experiences. The other culprits are silly colloquialisms we have in society, like, "It was just my eyes playing tricks on me" or "It was just a trick of the light."

Another way clairvoyance gets shut down is through ingesting fluoride. For most of my life, I believed Fluoride is good for dental health. I'm not a dentist, so do your own research. I've discovered fluoride is a neurotoxin that calcifies the pineal gland. The pineal gland is the physical gland in your brain connected to your Clairvoyance.

According to Healthline.com, when you ingest fluoride (either through your water or your toothpaste) on a regular basis, it's attracted to the calcium in your system. This can create a buildup of calcium deposits that prevent your pineal gland from functioning properly. As you're developing your Clairvoyance, you'll need to:

- Eliminate all sources of fluoride in your life
- Let go of all the colloquialism beliefs you've taken on
- Start to validate your visual intuition.

We will talk much more about validating your intuition in Step 4.

Are you a Primary Clairvoyant?

Here are four traits to determine if clairvoyance is your primary intuitive sense:

Vivid or Lucid Dreams

Someone who is Clairvoyant will already be having nightly dreams. You may not dream vividly every night, but every once in a while, you still have a dream you remember when you wake up. A dream that affects you and makes you wonder if it means anything.

You may even know it means something, but you're not exactly sure what. If you're Clairvoyant, you may have already experienced a lucid dream. A lucid dream is when you become aware that you're dreaming while you're in the dream. We'll dive deeper into dreams, dream work, and lucid dreams in Step 2.

Photographic Memory

If you're Clairvoyant, you will have somewhat of a photographic memory. You'll be able to recall visual details well. You'll be very astute at noticing details in the moment. You're very observant. Good at games like Where's Waldo, memory matching games, and Pictionary.

Visual Learner

Primary Clairvoyants are visual learners. You can take in information if a visual aid is present, like a poster or a teacher writing on a whiteboard. You're skilled at memorizing things like affirmations, poems, or lines for a play.

"A Creative"

If you're Clairvoyant, you may consider yourself to be a "creative." This doesn't have to mean that you are good at drawing and painting, although you might be. Creative pursuits include everything from:

- Visual art
- Cooking
- Arts and crafts
- Design
- Gardening
- Or simply a creative way of thinking.

If you can:

- Observe and notice details that others don't
- Adjust your mindset effectively
- Desire to live your life according to your joy and not the expectations of others

You are a "creative." In fact, every single human being is creative. You're co-creating your reality with Spirit in every moment.

Clairvoyance Quiz

Take this quiz to discover if Clairvoyance is your primary intuitive sense. After taking all four quizzes, compare your results to determine which Clair is your primary and which is your secondary.

If yes, put a 3. If sometimes, put a 2. If no, put a 1 in the box.

- You have vivid dreams every once in a while or did when you were a kid.
- You have a photographic memory and are very good at noticing visual details.
- You've always had an active imagination.
- You've seen lights or shadows out of the corner of your eye.
- You're a visual learner.

Clairvoyant Experience

Write 3-4 sentences in your journal or workbook about a dream that stuck out to you. What feeling did you have in/with the dream? What were the key visuals that you remember?

How to Activate Your Clairvoyance

Physical Organs

You need to know which physical organs are associated with your Clairvoyance. This is an easy way to figure out what's blocking full activation of your Clairvoyance. Any issues in these organs will point to energetic dysfunction within the chakra (third eye) connected to it.

I am not a medical doctor and do not claim to know how to heal these organs, body parts, or physical issues.

The physical organs and body parts linked to Clairvoyance are:

- Eyes
- Brain
- Pineal gland

Physical Issues

When you look at the above list of organs and body parts, do you have any issues or conditions within them? Things like:

- Glaucoma
- Cataracts
- Blindness, any level
- Needing glasses, contact lenses
- Migraines
- Headaches
- Strokes

- Seizures
- Mental disturbance or illness
  - Bipolar disorder
  - Schizophrenia
  - Depression
  - Anxiety
- Brain Tumors

Energetic Issues

These are the issues connected to dysfunction in the third eye chakra:

- Resistance to new ideas
- Resistance to change
- Feeling that your beliefs are the only "correct" beliefs
- Closed minded-ness
- Lack of self-awareness
- Trouble remembering your dreams
- Turning a "blind eye" to others
- Enabling others' addictions or negative behavior patterns
- Struggling to be creative or use your imagination

A note here is that as a natural empath, you may not struggle with many of the above energetic issues in the third eye. You could actually have an overactive third eye. This would have you projecting shadows onto others that you need to heal within yourself. You could even see someone as their best self instead of who they truly are in that moment. Cultivating self-awareness is a key to healing and activating your third eye.

Write your responses in your journal or workbook.

1. *Which energetic third eye issue hits deep?*

2. *Why do you think you struggle with this?*

3. *How can you change this?*

Extra Credit: Answer questions 2 and 3 for each energetic issue listed.

Heal Your Third Eye Chakra

Here are some tips on how to heal your third eye chakra:

- Honor your need for solitude

You need time and space to hear your own thoughts. To know your own mind and become aware of the patterns within it. Also, you can discern your own thoughts from the thoughts of those around you.

Take regular time to be by yourself, either in your home or nature, away from people and devices.

- Keep your spaces clean and organized

Your environment is a reflection of your mental state. If you're surrounded by clutter, staying calm, organized, and centered will be hard. Cultivate habits of decluttering, cleaning, and organization within your home. Outsource some help in that area if you have the ability.

- Meditation

Rest your mind and receive intuitive downloads through regular meditation. Don't panic! I'll dive into several types of meditation in Step 3, so you don't have to force yourself to sit in silence with a busy mind!

For a Third Eye Chakra Clear, Heal, & Power Up Guided Meditation, visit www.ciararubin.com/yakbookresources

- Dream Journaling

Dreams are a window into your subconscious and a path toward absolute self-awareness. I'll dive more into how to remember, journal, and interpret your dreams in Step 2.

- Color Therapy
  - Wear or surround yourself with indigo blue.
  - Create art with the color indigo blue.

REMINDER: There's a freaking awesome table containing all of the above information on Activating your Clairvoyance in an easy-to-read format at the end of the book.

Opening Your Third Eye

Because we're such a visual society, Clairvoyance is given a lot of clout and importance in the spiritual community. Clairvoyance is extremely valuable and magical! That being said, you may subconsciously fear your clairvoyance.

There are many energies, beings, and forms of Consciousness all around you at all times. It can be a little daunting and even scary to open your third eye but to access the full power of your clairvoyance, you'll need to.

When I was first reawakening my clairvoyance, I was terrified, worrying about what I'd see. I was already seeing shadow beings and full-bodied ghost apparitions. I was scared that once I opened my third eye, I'd be seeing legit demons.

There are indeed negative aspects of consciousness, but:

You have the choice of whether to focus on those negative aspects.

What you see and experience is directly related to your frequency and vibration.

Once you commit to your Shadow Work (which we'll talk about in Step 2), you'll be less likely to see scary things with every shadow you heal.

You can always set boundaries with Spirit and let your higher self know what you are and are unwilling to see. We'll talk more about setting boundaries in Step 3.

For now, the most important thing to know about opening your third eye is that it's all about becoming self-aware. Opening your third eye enables you to see into your subconscious. This, in turn, helps you to heal your shadows more completely. Being able to envision your inner workings is crucial to earning authentic respect.

If you're someone who wants to help people in some way, you'd better be helping yourself. If you want to help people see their own faults and limiting beliefs, you sure as hell better be looking at yours. I assure you that it is safe for you to be powerfully and profoundly clairvoyant.

For the See Good Things Guided Third Eye Opening Meditation, visit www.ciararubin.com/yakbookresources

Chapter 4:
Clairaudience

How it Works

Clairaudience means clear hearing. This intuitive sense centers in the throat chakra, as well as the smaller ear chakras. The throat chakra resonates with the color light blue.

See diagram.

Clairaudient information comes through your inner ear, where you'll hear sounds or voices inside your head. It also comes through your physical ears. You can express your clairaudience by:

- Speaking to yourself or others in your head

- Anytime you open your mouth and make physical sounds (speech, singing, etc.)

Clairaudience is all about hearing and expression. Clairaudience is a powerful yet often underutilized intuitive sense. Your hearing is so subtle and sensitive, especially when you're clairaudient.

Let's talk about the experience of receiving intuitive information via clairaudience.

Experiencing Clairaudience

Song Signs

You hear a song on the radio, or let's be real, your Spotify playlist, and you feel connected to it like it reflects a situation you're currently going through. That's a song sign. Song signs are your higher self queuing up a song to communicate with you.

Spirit and your higher self will always speak your language. It'll choose a song that fits your style and speaks to what you need to hear in that moment. If you like heavy metal, it'll be heavy metal. If you're into singer-songwriters, you'll hear them belt it out. These signs are indications that spirit is witnessing and supporting you. If this sounds awesome, or like it's happened to you before, you should start listening to music more often!

You'll even start having songs pop into your head at opportune moments. Don't discount this; it definitely means something! Pay attention to the lyrics and how the song makes you feel.

Disembodied sounds/music

You are surrounded by a field of energy and consciousness at all times. You are part of that field. Because of this, clairaudients will often experience disembodied sounds, voices, or even music. This means you will hear a sound with your physical ears that can't easily be explained away. You may hear a garbled conversation with no physical origin or explanation. You may have even experienced hearing someone calling your name when "no one is there."

If you've experienced this, don't be alarmed! You're tapping into the multidimensional universe expressed through sound. Your angels and Spirit guides, as well as departed loved ones, can be around you at any given time. If you're clairaudient, they may try to communicate with you through that intuitive sense.

Voices

I always tell my students and clients that it's okay to hear voices "as long as the voices aren't telling you to do anything bad to yourself or others." Sort of a dark joke, but I mean it! The experience of clairaudience will include hearing voices. Often, you will hear voices inside your head or your inner ear. Clairaudience centers in the throat chakra **and** the ear chakras. These voices are simply your higher self, Spirit guides, Source energy (or God), trying to communicate with you.

It's true that dark energies could be trying to communicate with you, but don't panic. In Step 3, we will dive into spiritual self-care and the practice of setting boundaries. Always remember: you are the master of this physical domain. No dark energies can harm you if you don't allow it.

Channeling

Clairaudience is not only about hearing but also expression. When most people think of channeling, they think of someone with their eyes closed, bringing through a message from:

- Spirits

- Ascended Masters

- Galactic beings

- Collective Consciousnesses.

This is only one aspect of channeling. Most people who experience channeling experience it as a flow state. That feeling when you lose track of time and are completely immersed in a task or project that brings you joy. Passion and inspiration expressing through you into whatever you're doing. Being present in the moment.

Are you a Primary Clairaudient?

Here are four traits that can help you determine if clairaudience is your primary intuitive sense.

Auditory Learner

If you consider yourself an auditory learner, you will have easier access to your clairaudience. Auditory learners are good at hearing information and memorizing it. They loved to be read to as a child and most likely still love reading.

Communicator

Primary clairaudients are natural communicators. They love to talk, express themselves, and often even love to hear the sound of their own voice, no shame! As a clairaudient, you're good at:

- Making connections with other people

- Engaging them in conversation

- Creating your own community or personal network

Teacher Type

The primary clairaudient is totally a teacher archetype. You're so good at absorbing information. You're able to translate that information and express it in a way that others can understand. You probably loved playing "school" (as the teacher, of course). You may even have loved many things about school itself. You're the teacher, counselor, or advice giver among your friends.

Musically Inclined

If you're clairaudient, you'll most likely be musically inclined. This can range all the way from:

- Writing or reading music

- Having mastered a certain musical instrument, like guitar, piano, or voice

All the way to being an avid music lover and listener.

You may have played an instrument as a child, or you may still be able to pick up an instrument and play it by ear. Clairaudients have a wide variety of tastes in music; they can appreciate many different genres.

Clairaudience Quiz

Take this quiz to discover if Clairaudience is your primary intuitive sense. After taking all four Clair quizzes, you'll compare your results and determine which Clair is your primary and which is your secondary.

If yes, put a 3. If sometimes/somewhat, put a 2. If no, put a 1 in the box.

- Are you an auditory learner?
- Do you love (like, really love) to teach and guide others?
- Are you musically inclined?
- Were you talkative as a child?
- Have you ever heard sounds/words/music that had no physical origin?

Clairaudient Experience

Write 3-4 sentences in your journal or workbook a song that means a lot to you. What are the lyrics of the song, and what is the overall message? How do you connect this song to your life?

How to Activate Your Clairaudience

Physical Organs

You need to know which physical organs are associated with your Clairaudience. This is an easy way to figure out what's blocking full activation of your Clairaudience. Any issues in these organs will point to energetic dysfunction within the chakra (throat) connected to it.

I am not a medical doctor and do not claim to know how to heal these organs, body parts, or physical issues.

The physical organs and body parts linked to Clairaudience are:

- Throat
- Neck
- Shoulders
- Mouth
- Tongue
- Teeth
- Gums
- Chin
- Jaw
- Sinuses
- Vocal Chords
- Esophagus
- Ears
- Thyroid

Physical Issues

When you look at the above list of organs and body parts, do you have any issues or conditions within them? Things like:

- Chronic bad breath or halitosis
- TMJ
- Tightness in the jaw or lockjaw
- Grinding the teeth
- Chronic sinus issues or allergies
- Tonsillitis
- Chronic strep or sore throat
- Stiff or sore neck or shoulders
- Neck or upper spinal issues or injuries
- Tooth decay
- Chronic cavities
- Root canals
- Thyroid issues
- Losing your voice (laryngitis, hoarseness)

Energetic Issues

These are the energetic issues connected to dysfunction in the throat chakra:

- Lying of any kind
  - Lying to protect yourself or someone else
  - Lying by omission

- White lies
- Anytime you're lying to yourself
- Being hushed or shamed for being talkative or loud
- Stifling of your creativity or creative impulse
- Fearing rejection for being yourself
- Not speaking your truth, not speaking up for what you want or believe
- Demanding what you want (from ego)
- Biting your tongue
- Swallowing your words
- Putting your foot in your mouth
- Being passive aggressive

Write your responses in your journal or workbook.

1. Which energetic throat issue hits deep?

2. Why do you think you struggle with this?

3. How can you change this?

Extra Credit: Answer questions 2 and 3 for each energetic issue listed.

Heal Your Throat Chakra

Here are some tips on how to heal your throat chakra:

- Journaling

I'll give you several ways to do this in Step 3.

- Chanting or Singing Meditation

For Mantra Chanting and Singing Guided Meditations, visit www.ciararubin.com/yakbookresources

For a Throat Chakra Clear, Heal, & Power Up Guided Meditation, visit www.ciararubin.com/yakbookresources

- Living, communicating, and acting within your highest truth

Or at least journeying toward this! It's a process, so don't be too hard on yourself. Start taking baby steps each day.

- Express yourself creatively

Find something creative that brings you joy! You don't have to be good at it!

- Express yourself honestly in healthy ways

Tell them how you really feel, but take a deep breath first.

- Color therapy
  - Wear or surround yourself with light blue.
  - Create art with the color light blue.

REMINDER: There's a freaking awesome table containing all of the above information on Activating your Clairaudience in an easy-to-read format at the end of the book.

Chapter 5:
Claircognizance

How it Works

Claircognizant means clear knowing or understanding. It centers in the crown chakra, all the way at the top of your head. The crown chakra resonates with the color violet.

See diagram.

Claircognizant information comes in through your brain. You'll sense thoughts that seem to come from somewhere else. They are, in fact, coming from your intuition and higher self. It will feel almost like an electric impulse.

Claircognizance is often one of the more elusive intuitive senses. This type of psychic information comes into your awareness fast and is quite subtle.

Let's talk about the experience of receiving intuitive information via claircognizance.

Experiencing Claircognizance

Thought > Contact

You're thinking of somebody, and then they contact you soon after. You may get an impulse to contact someone, and then when you do, they say something like, "I was just thinking about you!" Has this ever happened to you? It's your claircognizance at work!

Lightning-fast Knowing

Lightning-fast knowing is definitely the identifying characteristic for experiencing claircognizance. It's different from a knowing that you feel in your gut or body. It comes into your awareness like a freaking lightning bolt. You ask yourself a question, and immediately, you know the answer. The same can happen when someone else asks you a question. We often bypass this initial intuitive answer and give a more "diplomatic" response.

Most people have learned to ignore their claircognizant intuition because it can be direct. It can be very affronting and difficult for other people to take. Yet, our lives would benefit from some sincere and honest communication. It would prevent a lot of stress and inauthentic situations.

Thought Sensing

Claircognizance is all about thoughts and mental energy. So, sometimes, you can even experience sensing the actual thoughts of other people. This can sometimes get a little muddled with clairsentience. You may get a sense that someone is thinking something and then get a feeling that confirms that sense. Even if they say something counter to what you sense they're thinking.

A lot of this relates to what I spoke about above. When you get a lightning-fast knowing, you temper it into a more people-pleasing response. It's not usually fruitful to call people out on the thoughts you sense they're thinking. It will often shock them, and they'll deny it. Furthermore, they may not even be aware of their actual thoughts, so you wouldn't be able to "get through to them."

Thought sensing is especially prevalent between people who are super close, like:

- Twins

- Spouses

- Best friends

- Especially in the mother-child relationship.

Telepathy

Telepathy is the ability to communicate with another person through your thoughts. This experience of claircognizance is pretty rare in society today! This is because most people aren't aware of the fact that they are more than just their thoughts. They don't have an awareness of or trust in their claircognizance and haven't spent much time developing their intuition.

That said, telepathy is an ability that every human being can cultivate. In today's world, most people are so caught up in their emotional pain. They are unaware that they're operating from that unresolved emotional pain. This is another reason telepathy isn't happening as much, which could be a good thing for now!

As more people learn to love themselves and heal, we will experience telepathy on a societal scale. For now, this happens most often with twins, very close siblings, and in the mother-child relationship. It can also happen in other relationships, but those are the most common.

Are You a Primary Claircognizant?

Here are four traits to help you determine if claircognizance is your primary intuitive sense.

Intellectual

The primary claircognizant is at least somewhat, if not quite intellectual. Claircognizants have a thirst for knowledge, unlike most other people. If this is your primary sense, you may resonate with the label bookworm or teacher's pet. You might have shame around this or try to pretend you're not as smart as you are so you "fit in" and don't get made fun of. I hope you know this is a powerful and important part of who you are.

Intuitive Family

Claircognizants have one or more of their other intuitive senses already turned on. Most claircognizants have spent other lifetimes developing and perfecting their intuition. Someone who's claircognizant will have grown up in a very intuitive family.

It may have been spoken or unspoken, but you will know what I'm talking about if this is true for you. Even if you grew up in a religious household, you could have been in a very intuitive family. Religion is a man-made construct to explain the spirituality that comes from within. Being religious doesn't mean you can't be intuitive. Remember, intuition and being psychic or intuitive are part of being human.

Extensive Knowledge of Symbols

Claircognizant information tends to come in as symbols. Someone with a knowledge and understanding of symbols and symbolism is claircognizant. If you love reading and are good at connecting the dots in a way other people can't, claircognizance is your primary intuitive sense.

Claircognizance Quiz

Take this quiz to discover if Claircognizance is your primary intuitive sense. After taking all four Clair quizzes, compare your results and determine which Clair is your primary and which is your secondary.

If yes, put a 3. If sometimes/somewhat, put a 2. If no, put a 1 in the box.

Are you a bit of a nerd?

Do you come from an intuitive family?

Have you ever thought about someone, and then they contacted you?

You love exploring symbolism and metaphor.

Have you ever had the experience of "just knowing" something that ended up being spot on?

Claircognizant Experience

Write 3-4 sentences in your journal or workbook about a symbol that's very meaningful to you and what it represents for you in your life.

How to Activate Your Claircognizance

Physical Organs

You need to know which physical organs are associated with your Claircognizance. This is an easy way to figure out what's blocking full activation of your Claircognizance. Any issues in these organs will point to energetic dysfunction within the chakra (crown) connected to it.

I am not a medical doctor and do not claim to know how to heal these organs, body parts, or physical issues.

The physical organs and body parts linked to Claircognizance are:

- Brain
- Pineal gland
- Pituitary gland
- Hypothalamus
- Central nervous system

Physical Issues

When you look at the above list of organs and body parts, do you have any issues or conditions within them? Things like:

- Anxiety
- Fears within your mind
- Bipolar
- Depression
- Insomnia

- ADHD
- Headaches
- Strokes
- Brain Tumors
- Epilepsy
- Parkinson's
- Alzheimer's
- Dementia

Energetic Issues

These are the issues connected to dysfunction in the crown chakra:

- Trauma-informed belief systems (we'll dive deeper into this in Step 2)
- Fear
- Breaking of trust or mistrust
- This can manifest as others betraying you and is usually a reflection of how you feel about God, Spirit, and yourself.
- Feeling disconnected from God, Source energy, the Universe, and/or your spirituality
- Thinking that your beliefs are the only "right ones"
  - Do you hold too tightly to your beliefs, or do you allow them to change as you learn and grow?
- Do you believe you are connected to and live in a supportive Universe?

Write your responses in your journal or workbook.

1. Which energetic crown issue hits deep?

2. Why do you think you struggle with this?

3. How can you change this?

Extra Credit: Answer questions 2 and 3 for each energetic issue listed.

Heal Your Crown Chakra

Here are some tips on how to heal your crown chakra:

- Examine your beliefs and belief systems on the reg.

Leave behind the beliefs that no longer serve you or your highest good (I'll show you how in Step 2!).

- What beliefs might be holding you back?

- Where did those beliefs come from?

- Cultivate mindfulness

  - Self-awareness

  - Gratitude

- Release attachment to specific outcomes

Easier said than done!

For the Let it TF Go Meditation, visit www.ciararubin. com/yakbookresources

- Surrendering to divine will and divine timing.

Trust the timing. You'll never get something you can't handle, and nothing that's meant for you will pass you by. See the above meditation link for letting it TF go.

- Release your need to control others.

Control is an illusion. Set boundaries, limits, and guidelines. If they're not respected, try again. If they're still not respected, leave the relationship or go get some counseling.

- Meditation (obvi!)

For a Crown Chakra Clear, Heal, & Power Up Guided Meditation, visit www.ciararubin.com/yakbookresources

- Color Therapy

  - Wear or surround yourself with purple.

  - Create art with the color purple.

REMINDER: There's a freaking awesome table containing all of the above information on Activating your Claircognizance in an easy-to-read format at the end of the book.

Quiz Results

Bring it all together to determine your primary and secondary intuitive senses!

Add up your scores! The highest number will be your primary intuitive sense. The second highest will be your secondary sense. Write them here:

Primary:

Secondary:

Are you surprised? Or did you already have a feeling?

Chapter 6:
You Are All the Clairs

We all love to fit into a labeled box that we can check off. We love to understand and describe things with our logical brains. Figuring out which intuitive sense is your primary and/or secondary appeals to you (it appeals to me, too). This is why systems like Myers-Briggs, the Enneagram, Astrology, and Human Design are such attractive and powerful tools.

It's understandable because the more you know yourself, the easier it is to move through life in an authentic way. Co-creating your life becomes a more joyful experience. You're creating a life you desire instead of the life someone else told you you should create. Or the life you feel you should create based on other people's expectations or what's worked well for them.

All that said, it's important for me to let you know that you have access to all four of these psychic senses. You are all the Clairs. You may have one or two that are more pronounced. As you move through this book, you'll find that all four of the intuitive senses will come into focus.

As you follow the system and steps I've laid out, all your Clairs will begin to develop holistically. This is how it was (and still is) for me, and this is the goal. When it comes to your physical senses, you have all five of them (ideally), and the intuitive senses are the same way.

The clearer each Clair becomes, the more you'll trust it. The less attached you'll be to which way or through which chakra the information is coming in. All that matters is that messages from God, your angels, your guides, or your higher self are available. And that you're capable of sensing and interpreting that information. As you start to trust and live from your intuition, your life will improve in every area. Relationships, friendships, opportunities, money, all of it!

Everyone is Psychic

I mentioned this earlier and want to help it hit home for you. Everyone is intuitive and has the ability to become psychic. A "psychic" embraces their intuitive abilities and uses them in their daily lives and on their career path.

You don't have to be "born with it" because everyone is born with it. You don't have to be a 4th-generation psychic or a third-generation witch; witchcraft has nothing to do with it. Intuitive abilities are your birthright. They are the next level of your human evolution. To help you move from a state of mere survival into the thriving full expression of your capabilities.

Some people may use these abilities for good, to serve others, and some may use them only to serve themselves. Psychic abilities are simply a tool we have in our human toolbox; they're not inherently good or bad.

No one is left out of this equation. Not you, not your family members, not the people of the third world, and not even the corrupt politicians. That said, everyone has the choice of whether to develop these abilities. Some people are so attached to their fear that they'll never fully realize their potential. Some believe they're utilizing their abilities, but true clarity does not come without Shadow Work. We'll dive into Shadow work in the next part of the book.

WTF is a Higher Self?

Your higher self is your soul. Let me give you a visual. Imagine an onion with its many layers. Each layer of the onion represents one of your lives or incarnations on this planet (or others). You could have hundreds or even thousands of layers in your onion, representing the age of your soul. I'm certain you're an old soul. Now imagine there is a giant skewer stabbing through the center of the onion. This skewer represents your soul or higher self. This is who you truly are.

Your higher self is this part of you existing in all your incarnations. In all time periods since the beginning of your soul's journey. That moment when your soul splits off from its oversoul and Source or God. The perspective of your higher self, is one you can trust. This is because your higher self exists outside of time and has no fear. Your higher self is unconditionally loving, compassionate, wise, and supportive of you. As you read the rest of this book, use this definition and understanding of your higher self.

The "Special Shadow"

This may or may not resonate with you. But it was a part of my journey, so I want to mention it here for all the light workers reading this book (hey girl! I see you!). When I first started awakening to my psychic abilities, I felt so validated.

Growing up, I never felt like I fit in; no one ever understood me. So, when I finally understood that I never fit in because I was born to stand out, it was definitely an ego trip. I felt super special and gifted with powerful abilities.

These feelings are contrary to my message that you read earlier. I came to the realization that everyone was psychic pretty early on in my work, and when I did- I built my first website. But before that, I definitely got off on feeling more special than others. Like all my childhood suffering and pain was because of my true "superiority."

This is a shadowy belief that is rampant within the spiritual community. Many spiritual teachers and leaders relish in self-importance over the fact that their abilities began in childhood. Some feel that they're special channels of information that others can't access. All this sits within an unhealed "specialness shadow."

I have compassion for those under this veil; if you're one of them, you may feel triggered right now. It's very important to understand that our job here on Earth is to help humanity to the point where we're no longer needed. For most everyone to be self-loving and powerful. How can we ever complete our mission if we claim or feel more gifted than everyone else?

It's true; you may be more spiritually skilled than others. This is because of the other lifetimes you've lived and the amount of work you do on yourself and your intuition. But these are skills that anyone can learn. For humanity to realize its full potential, we as spiritual teachers and leaders must let go of needing to be more psychic.

I'd like you to journal on this topic. Explore which childhood wounds may contribute to this feeling of needing so deeply to be seen and validated by others in these ways.

WERK.

I hope you feel self-empowered and excited by this new or deeper understanding of your intuition. As you continue to move through this book, your intuitive abilities and spiritual experiences will grow.

We've explored your intuition and how your intuitive information is coming in. Now, it's time to clear your energy so that the full expression of your intuition can come into focus. Only then will you be able to trust it enough to make small and big decisions from that place. Girl, you betta shadow WERK.

STEP 2:
Releasing Fear

Chapter 7:
I Came Outta the Spiritual Closet

I came out of the spiritual closet on Facebook by accident! I was taking a card reading course online. I posted a beautiful picture of a 3-card reading I'd done for homework (complete with crystals and candles). I talked about my interpretation of the reading. How I needed to follow my purpose and path as an intuitive and spiritual teacher. Then I hit *Post*.

I thought it would be private in the card reading course group, but it wasn't! Family members, friends, and even people I worked with at the Chamber of Commerce started liking the post. Most people didn't say anything to my face, but a few people started asking for readings!

As I gained more and more knowledge and understanding, it became harder and harder to go to work every day. I knew that I wasn't helping anybody and contributing to an organization built on ego. I told my boss to his face that I was quitting to become a psychic. In his wide-eyed, politically correct way, he responded, "Help me understand that." (LOL) I gave them a full month's notice and even trained my replacements.

Once free of the 9 to 5, I spent two months crumpled in a pile of tears and tissues on my couch. I put myself through what I now call the "Healing Gauntlet." This was my first real experience with Shadow Work. I wouldn't recommend doing this, though it was effective. I was digging and looking for any Shadows I could heal.

Any dysfunctional behaviors I had, fixing my diet, forgiving ex-boyfriends and ex-friends. Healing my inner child. Constant reflecting on painful memories. Feeling emotions I'd never let myself feel, letting it all out. After 2 months of this, I had a profound mystical experience.

As usual, I was lying on the couch in the middle of the day. I'd fallen asleep after a particularly intense sobbing session. I started dreaming, though I seemed to be right in the spot where I had fallen asleep. I call this type of dream the "in-between."

As I looked around, a bolt of lightning seemed to come through the ceiling, hitting me right in the heart. I wouldn't say it was painful, but it was definitely a very intense and "assertive" feeling. Like shock waves moving through my entire body, making my arms and legs convulse wildly. This "lightning activation" seemed to last for at least 45 to 60 Seconds. Finally, it stopped and left me limp on the couch, still in the "dream."

As I lay there, I felt completely fried. One more breath and I was being levitated off the couch. I remember being in the dream and thinking, "Am I levitating? Am I doing this, or is someone or something else controlling this?"

As I lifted higher and higher toward the ceiling, a silver pool of light appeared above me. I closed my eyes and heard the words "Christlight" whispered into my ear as I passed into the pool. Not much time to contemplate the strangeness of this as I was confronted with the feeling of being inside this silver pool of light. It felt completely healing, cooling, and warm at the same time. It felt as though I was one with it. Like I no longer had a body. It felt Divine, especially after the whole lightning episode. After what felt like another 45 to 60 seconds, I was lowered back down to the couch.

Next, still in the "dream," I noticed my husband Zach sitting on the couch near me. I sat up and was about to tell him about the experience I'd had when he said, "The Galactic Federation is here now. You'll be hearing from them very soon. It's time to begin." And with that, I woke up.

The entire experience floored me. I know that clearing my body and energy field of so much Shadow at one time created the ability to handle that experience. I'd lightened enough of my density to be able to withstand some type of massive light activation.

It's very important for me to state right here and now that this "activation" wasn't my goal while healing. Also, anyone and everyone can achieve and create the possibility for their own light activation should they choose. You do not need anyone to activate you, and you do not need anyone to heal you. This is actually not possible. You are the only one who can achieve activation when you are ready, and only you and your higher self will know when you're ready.

You are also the only one who can heal yourself. Other healers can hold and provide space and facilitate your healing. But you are the only one doing the actual healing. Please commit this truth into your heart and soul. If someone claims to be able to heal or activate you, this is their ego talking. No matter how experienced they are, how famous they are, or how powerful they seem.

If the experience I described doesn't sound desirable, don't worry; your experience will be exactly what is meant for you. And if you don't want a massive light activation, don't put yourself through a healing gauntlet.

There are many ways to do Shadow Work; you can face it in big bursts or let things come up naturally. Now that you've heard some of my first experiences with Shadow Work, let's dive in. It's time to learn about this amazing, life-changing, intuition-accelerating practice. Shadow Work is still somewhat new in the spiritual community, and it's a practice that many people either skip or resist.

I'm not going to sugarcoat it for you. Shadow Work is work, and it's hard and messy. That's why I'm simplifying Shadow Work for you. I'll give you step-by-step instructions so you'll feel supported in your healing and awakening process.

I know that you came here at this time for a reason. You have something to say, something to share with others. You're reading this book because you want to develop and trust your intuition, which is a part of you. And so, you need to develop your relationship with your full self and trust yourself enough to make decisions that might feel risky.

You need Shadow Work to make the decisions that will move you onto the trajectory you want for your life. Walking your talk with integrity isn't possible without Shadow work. Please take my hand and walk with me, not over or around, but through the darkness. Let my light be your guide so you can remember and shine yours as bright as possible.

I'll teach you what shadows are, how they wreak havoc in your life, and how to heal them. Let's dive in!

Chapter 8:
What are Shadows?

Shadows are limiting beliefs that you may or may not be aware of. These limiting beliefs develop as a result of trauma. These traumas could be big or small. It could have happened in childhood, adolescence, adulthood, or even in other lifetimes. You'll know you have them because they'll connect to dysfunctional behaviors.

A few examples of dysfunctional Behavior:

- Saying yes to something and then feeling resentful while completing that thing.

Your resentment could even result in you low-key lashing out at others for feeling drained. You had the choice to say no in the first place. This dysfunctional behavior is usually the result of people pleasing and fear of abandonment. Two issues that often plague empaths. So you say yes when you don't mean it. You believe this will make you valuable, loved, or accepted.

- Ghosting somebody, aka completely cutting off contact with someone without warning. Not responding to their calls or messages, and moving on with your life (so to speak) without them in it.

While some people are toxic, most at least deserve a process of you slowly drawing boundaries with them. You can do this until the relationship is one you feel more comfortable with. They may even leave on their own because they no longer have the access to your energy that they need to maintain their own dysfunction.

It can be difficult to self-examine and acknowledge that you have dysfunctional behaviors. We're all doing the best we can with the understanding that we have. So, being self-critical like this can be painful and taken too far if you're not careful. You're human, and it's human to make mistakes.

Limiting beliefs is what you believe about yourself, others, and the world. They're limiting your full self-realization and self-actualization. Limiting beliefs are most often living in your subconscious mind. You could say they're hidden from the light of your understanding and awareness. For this reason, these limiting beliefs are your darkness or shadow side.

Understanding how your Shadows affect you in your day-to-day life is important.

What Shadows Do

For you to understand how Shadows affect you in your life, I'm going to use an analogy of goggles. Each dysfunctional behavior and limiting belief is a shadow. Imagine each Shadow as one pair of goggles. As you move through your childhood and adult life, you experience traumas, either small or big. With each trauma, you develop a limiting belief or a new pair of goggles. By the time you start your Shadow Work journey, you may have collected dozens or even 50 pairs of goggles. This prevents you from clearly seeing yourself, others, and the world.

When you can't see things clearly, making intuitive decisions is hard. This lack of clarity is what creates the same frustrating situations for you over and over again. In your relationships, jobs, and life in general. You keep making decisions informed by your shadows, so you're living a life-limiting your full potential.

Further to that point, your experience of reality is directly related to the amount of shadow within you. I mean literally:

- The way you perceive people

- The kinds of experiences that you're having in your day-to-day life

- The actual reality you are co-creating with Spirit

All this is because of your frequency, your vibration, and the energy you're putting out based on your beliefs. I'm not saying those other people aren't toxic. But the way you're interacting with them and how they can trigger you are because of your shadows. If you've experienced a lot of trauma, you're not seeing the world or yourself in a true way.

As you start to do Shadow Work, you begin to remove pairs of goggles. Depending on how deep you go and how completely you practice Shadow Work, You could even be removing several pairs of goggles at once. Through this process, you will start to see yourself and the world as it truly is. I had a very interesting mystical experience that taught me this lesson.

I set the intention to open my third eye, even though I was afraid of what I'd see. And my fear was confirmed with Banshees. I started seeing Banshees all the time whenever I was home. A Banshee is a negative female spirit. These banshees were disturbing to witness. They looked like that girl from *The Ring* movie: slender with dark hair, a gaunt-looking face, and sunken eyes. I'd see one whenever I looked in the mirror and sense them whenever I was outside in the woods. It totally freaked me out.

In 2016, I went to a spiritual retreat in Egypt. While I was there, I had a whole host of mystical experiences, but one of them was seeing the "White Watchers." I was lying in bed one morning in my hotel room, in that space where you're about to wake up after having been asleep. Within the darkness behind my eyelids, I saw the stark contrast of an all-white being in my mind's eye.

This being was a tall humanoid figure, but definitely not human. He had huge black eyes, and it almost seemed like he was wearing some type of helmet with shields covering them. These shields made his eyes look even bigger than they actually were. His energy was very calm, stern, and yet benevolent and intelligent. I heard him in my mind's ear say, "We are the Watchers." In my head, I asked back, "Why are you here?" He said simply, "To watch."

He then explained that this was the purpose of his kind. To watch humans, humanity at large, and many other races throughout the Galaxy. To take this "recorded video footage" and broadcast it to anyone who wanted to learn about Earth and humanity. There are many beings interested in the "Earth Channel" right now.

All this seemed kind of creepy but also true, the way things are. I had a few more experiences with these types of beings while in Egypt, but I didn't think much about them once I got home. A few days after settling back home, I realized I was no longer seeing the Banshees. I looked for them, but they weren't there. But, I was seeing these white Watchers on my property. After a day of this, I asked one of the white Watcher beings where the Banshees had gone and why they were there instead. One of them matter-of-factly said, "We've always been here. You haven't been able to see us because of your fear."

In other words, the Banshees I was seeing were actually them the whole time. There was never an evil spirit following me around. I was perceiving things in that way because of a shadow I hadn't healed yet. I was able to take off enough pairs of goggles that I was seeing my reality in a truer, more positive light. Instead of being haunted by a cursed woman, I was actually the curiosity of galactic beings.

As you heal and change your vibration, the things you see and experience will change. Your perspective will change, so you'll start living from a new, higher perspective.

Why Heal Shadows?

Now you understand what Shadows do. How they hold you back and even change your perception and experience of reality. Let's dive into some even more obvious reasons why healing Shadows is so important. This motivation will help you muster the courage to embark on your Shadow Work journey.

Relationships

Shadow Work will improve every single relationship in your life. Struggles with your significant other will become easier to deal with. That's not to say they'll resolve instantly. You have to do the work, but I've experienced the results of this firsthand. The more Shadow Work I do, the better wife I become and the closer my husband and I are.

Then, there are difficult family relationships. The people that really push your buttons. Shadow Work will help you remove those buttons one by one. No matter what toxic bullshit they might be spreading, it's not going to bother you. This may seem hard to believe, but I've experienced it firsthand. My Shadow Work frees me from being ensnared by even the most narcissistic people in my family.

When it comes to friendships, Shadow Work will help you release the people from your life who aren't in your corner. The users and the energy vampires. Shadow Work will create space in your life for people more aligned with who you want to become. The truer version of yourself. People who motivate and inspire you instead of those who aren't happy about your successes.

Career/Life Purpose

Maybe you love what you do, maybe you hate it. I know you have at least a low-key desire to build something from your own creativity. To have your own business or, at the very least, freedom. Financial freedom, freedom to do what you want with your time. These are the things that make life as a human infinitely more enjoyable and fulfilling. Healing your shadows will shorten the time it takes to get to your goals.

Shadow energy takes up space in your mind. It blocks your ability to receive information from your intuition on your best next steps. If you're reading this book, it means that you have an important life purpose. All empaths have a mission in this world. This mission, this life purpose, is a spiritual calling. I know how satisfying it is to help other people. To feel as though you are making an impact and a difference in other people's lives. If this is in your heart, it's meant for you. Healing your shadows is the key to clearly seeing the path in front of you or at least the next few steps.

Opportunities

This may seem redundant, but I want to hammer this point home. There are opportunities all around you right now. Opportunities for more aligned relationships and friendships. Opportunities to make more money. When your limiting beliefs are active, it prevents you from seeing these opportunities. Or you're getting opportunities, but then they fizzle out or don't turn out the way you'd hoped. Shadow Work is the remedy.

Timelines

This topic is a bit more esoteric but very important, and I know you'll find it interesting. At this very moment, you are living and playing out a certain timeline. This timeline is on a trajectory based on your beliefs and also your soul contract. Aka, the things you agreed to take part in before you came into this life.

When it comes to timelines for your life, there are infinite possibilities. Every:

- Decision you make

- Feeling you feel or don't feel

- Even every thought you think (don't get too in your head about it!)

Puts you into another parallel timeline. Based on your current timeline, certain types of experiences, opportunities, and relationships will manifest in your life.

Challenges are important for teaching you what you don't prefer and helping you empower yourself. Of course, they're not always ideal and can often be toxic. As you start to do Shadow Work, the challenges you face become less challenging. This is because you have better tools to deal with them. The relationships that plagued you either fall away or become much more manageable. The opportunities you attract fall more in line with your true desires and bigger goals.

Shifting timelines is something that you're doing every day without even being aware of it. This isn't something to get all in your head about and overthink every thought. It's more something to be aware of on a peripheral level. Shadow Work is the only permanent way to shift to a timeline that brings you the most fulfillment.

Chapter 9:
The Low-Hanging Fruit

When you're doing Shadow work, go for the low-hanging fruit. These are the obvious elements of dysfunction in different parts of your life.

When I first started Shadow work, my ex-boyfriends were the low-hanging fruit. You'll know what that low-hanging fruit is for you. It could be ex-partners, a difficult family relationship, or a difficult work situation.

After years of Shadow Work, I noticed that my life was still lacking in the area of female friendship. This was something I'd struggled with since around age 12. I was carrying a story (limiting belief) that I just couldn't have friends. That no one other than my husband would ever put as much effort into the relationship as I would.

Funnily enough, I was super judgy of any female friend I would have. I'd often engage in the narcissistic practice of love bombing, isolating, and ghosting each friend I had. Eventually, I had several friends do the same thing to me.

As I started to awaken, I changed many of my interests and smaller personality traits. My old friends didn't resonate with how spiritual I'd become. The version of myself I was while friends with them was not actually true to who I am. It was the old version of me they signed up for. Once I started becoming who I am, they couldn't take it and ghosted me.

Real talk, as you do Shadow Work, this is a very real possibility. The people who leave you as you peel away layers of limiting beliefs are not the people meant to be in your life. The people who truly love and celebrate your success will stand by you.

No matter how much Shadow Work you do, you'll never change the core of who you are. Your interests and hobbies may shift. Your career path will likely change. I don't want you to fear these changes. Embrace them because you're changing into the person you came here to be. You're healing yourself and your ancestral line with every shadow you face.

If people leave your life, they don't truly love you. They were only connecting with you on superficial things or through a trauma bond. When they leave you, it creates space, time, and energy for relationships that will honor you. Relationships that will energize and inspire you. Rather than ones that drain you and cause drama.

At this point in my life, I've come so far in the area of female friendships. I've stopped ghosting people that don't deserve it. I keep good people in my life even if certain personality traits or parts of them no longer resonate with me. I set boundaries instead of cutting people out. I'm proud to say that my life is now full of inspiring, energizing, powerful spiritual women.

Facing Fears

As you start facing your shadows and becoming aware of any limiting beliefs you have, you'll run into fear. Fear is the opposite of love. It holds an energy of tension and anxiety. It can be expressed as anger, frustration, or straight-up paranoia. Fear is usually nothing more than a resistance to love. This resistance is an expression of beliefs you developed to survive.

While on your Shadow Work journey, your conscious fears are a great place to look. What are you afraid of? Why are you afraid of that thing? Was it someone else's fear they projected onto you, or was it a traumatic experience you had with that thing? Your fears often hold the keys and clues to your greatest powers and gifts.

Your fears also hold deep meaning. If you're afraid of snakes or spiders, look up the spiritual meaning of those creatures. If you're afraid of making a mess, why might that be? What's the worst thing that could happen if you got a little messy? These are all important questions that we will explore more at the end of this section of the book. Being willing to face your fears will bring you massive confidence.

You could journal on what would happen if you encountered that fear or situation. You could even practice some low-key or legit exposure therapy. Exposing yourself to things you're afraid of little by little will help reduce fear's power over you. You can work with random fears! You'll still find that:

- Your anxiety goes down,

- Your ability to tolerate stress goes up

- You're able to hear and interpret your intuition much more clearly.

In my experience, you don't have to face fears in a specific area of life you're trying to improve to improve it.

For example, I have this terrible fear of spilling my drink, especially if I've just finished making it. It's connected to my perfectionism and fear of making a mess or mistake. On a few occasions, I've made it a practice to purposefully spill a brand-new cup of tea. Then, I can witness the fear and talk myself through it with awareness.

Allowing myself to get a little messy shows me that making mistakes will not make me lose the ability to create and produce successful outcomes. This is powerful because it means I don't lose my shit when things start going wrong. I'm able to remain the eye of the storm. Processing my emotions with awareness while still moving forward toward my goals.

Face Your Fears

What are you afraid of, or what makes you cringe inside? Write in your journal or workbook two things that come to mind and look up their symbolic meanings. Free write to discover why you fear them and how you plan to overcome that fear.

Inner Child Work

When you dive into the world of shadows, inner child work will come up. So many of your beliefs formed in childhood, usually before the age of 10. Limiting beliefs are most often linked to traumatic experiences from childhood.

Inner child work is not about blaming your parents, society, or systemic issues. Those entities may well be responsible for the trauma you've experienced. Yet, taking ownership of your dysfunctional behaviors is what creates change.

Early on in my journey, I stumbled across the truth that we all choose the situations we are born into. Your higher self chose the family you were going to be born to. Your higher self chose the circumstances you were going to grow up with in your soul contract. A soul contract is an energetic contract you co-wrote before incarnating into your current body.

Why the hell would anyone choose all the bullshit you went through? Simple. Self-empowerment. You chose the parents who would trigger your deepest wounds, so you will be unstoppable once you overcome those wounds. You chose your unique situations so that you could see the depths of pain and come out the other side into the light.

Your trauma holds your greatest power. As a child, your experiences may have taught you not to trust others or yourself. These core wounds (once healed) hold the keys to your magic. Your intuition guides you into the darkness, so don't avoid it. Trust it

Triggers

Triggers are what happens and what people do that piss you off. Get your blood boiling and make you want to react (instead of responding). Your triggers are excellent indicators of shadows that need attention and healing.

Furthermore, there are two reasons someone will trigger you. Either they are:

- Exhibiting a trait you wish you had. Something that's possible for you but you haven't empowered yourself to yet.

- Exhibiting a toxic trait that you have but either don't like about yourself or don't want to admit you have it. They may be amplifying that toxic trait, yet it still lives within you.

This can be difficult to accept. But there is so much empowerment here. Cultivate awareness of who and what triggers you. You'll gain control over your life and its direction in a much bigger way.

Here's a super effective, quick, and easy exercise to do when triggered.

When You're Triggered by a Person or Situation

Their Name:

What You Like (about them/it)

What You Don't Like (about them/it)

After filling this out, decide:

- If you're triggered because they're doing something you wish you did or have something you wish you had?

  - Ask yourself why you think that trait or thing you're jealous of isn't possible for you?

  - Also, ask yourself how you can put yourself more in alignment with that trait or thing.

- If you're triggered because of their negative trait or dysfunctional behavior?
  - Take a moment to self-reflect and notice the times you may be exhibiting this trait or behavior.
  - Although this person may have the trait or behavior 10 or 20x more than you do, it's still something you do/have.
  - Ask yourself how you can go about either changing or accepting this trait or behavior within you.

Feel free to create one of these each time you're triggered!

Forgiveness

Let's get controversial. Bold statement: if you can't forgive, you will never truly be free of the negative energy that shackles you.

Forgiveness is not about condoning the negative actions, shitty behaviors, or toxic traits. Forgiveness is about setting yourself free. Deciding that you are worthy of being free of the negative emotions.

I'm not invalidating your trauma here. I understand what it's like to be betrayed, abandoned, and abused. It's terrible and terrifying. Yet you can choose to see how these things happened **for** you and not to you. You can start to separate the trauma from the specific person or people it came from.

Hurt people will hurt people. Holding on to righteous anger or unforgiveness is like drinking poison and expecting them to die. Your anger, disdain, disgust, or even indifference toward them will not change them. It won't show them the error of their ways. They may be choosing to hold on to their toxic traits, to remain unconscious and unaware of their problems. But you can choose differently.

Remember that unity consciousness is the ultimate truth. That at one level, we are one with one another. When you choose not to forgive someone who has wronged you, ultimately, you're choosing not to forgive yourself.

Stop punishing yourself with unforgiveness. You do not deserve to be punished. No matter what you've done or haven't done, you deserve to be free. Forgiveness isn't a linear path. Sometimes, it can be hard to know how to even begin to forgive. You don't have to know how. All you have to do is be willing. That willingness is an intention that your intuition, higher self, and Spirit or God can work with. As soon as you open up, Spirit will begin to manifest and show you the breadcrumbs you need to follow to forgive.

Seeing someone's wounded inner child and why they act/ acted the way they do/did will help you have compassion for them. You can choose to become aware of how they trigger you and either accept or change those traits.

Seriously, forgiveness is the key. Forgiveness is the only real and permanent way we will heal our shadows and move forward as a humanity. I'm not saying there aren't things in the world that need to change. But so often, we think that other people are the ones who need to change. That harmony will happen when the people we're pointing fingers at change and become aware.

The only person you can actually change is yourself. You can only inspire others to change. Transformation is your calling.

The more you transform your negativity and shadows into light, the more you forgive, and the more it actually changes others.

I've seen this from personal experience. When I've chosen to forgive someone who either did or didn't "deserve it," it's almost as if they changed. I'm not sure if they actually changed. Or if it was just me and my perspective of them that changed. Either way, my life has gotten easier every time and every person I've chosen to forgive. In my life today, I experience much less conflict and drama.

So the real question when you're feeling resistance to forgiving someone or something is: why am I holding on to this drama? What are my beliefs surrounding this situation? Why do I believe holding onto anger and/or resentment will improve the situation?

Like I said, forgiveness is (somehow weird, right?) a very controversial idea. Some people were even crucified for spreading the good word. That's my forgiveness soapbox; thank you very much!

Radical Personal Responsibility

Radical personal responsibility is a perspective that has brought me massive empowerment. I use the word radical because I apply this concept to absolutely everything. Without radical personal responsibility, your Shadow work will be ineffective.

Radical personal responsibility means:

You co-create every experience with the Source, God, or the Universe.

Every positive experience and every negative experience. You are not "to blame" for the bad things that have happened to you. You are not to blame, yet you are responsible for facing and healing those things. You're the only one who can change in any given situation. You can't change others. You can change your perspective, and you can change your actions.

Your higher self will manifest negative situations into your life until you're brave enough to:

- Face it with a self-aware mind

- Do your Shadow Work

- Heal that part of yourself so you no longer experience those same traumas.

Before you came into this life, you agreed to certain experiences that your soul wanted to learn from. From the Soul's perspective, there is no such thing as "bad experiences." The soul's deepest desire is to experience everything it can. The soul looks forward to negative and challenging experiences. Negative and challenging experiences teach you the most about yourself. Adversity, limitation, and challenge are often the fastest and deepest ways to find out who you are.

Even though you don't "deserve" the bad things that happen to you, you still manifest them. This perspective is empowering. If you're creating the experiences you don't like, it also means you have the power to stop those experiences from happening. I understand that you might be feeling some resistance to this concept. I still have moments of resistance to taking responsibility for my experiences.

I want to make it clear that you are not responsible for the actions of other people. This is not about sticking out in toxic situations because "you manifested it."

Radical personal responsibility is about:

- Accepting your power to create all situations you find yourself in

- Taking an honest look at why you may have attracted those situations

- Healing and setting boundaries accordingly

Take this concept with you through the rest of your life and the rest of this book.

Chapter 10:
Your Feminine and Masculine Energy

Every person has both feminine and masculine energies. Whether you're a man or a woman, you contain both energies inside you at varying levels of balance and harmony.

That said, each person will have a unique balance of these energies. As long as you're in harmony with yourself and your partner to the point where you can manifest all your desires, that's the most important thing.

Characteristics

Here are the general characteristics of the feminine and masculine archetypes:

Feminine Energy	Masculine Energy
• Rest	• Action
• Surrender, Allowing	• Control, Follow through
• Receiving	• Giving
• Flow	• Structure
• Unity	• Sovereignty
• Art	• Science
• Intuition	• Logic
• Darkness	• Light
• The Moon	• The Sun

What Balance Looks Like

You'll feel freedom and inner peace when your feminine and masculine energies are in balance. You'll be consistently productive without burning out. You'll allow and attract all your desires into your life exactly when you need them.

Your life will be rich with loving, healthy friendships, and you'll have amazing sex with your partner (no matter how long you've been together)! You'll feel creatively fulfilled and intellectually stimulated. Sounds freaking fantastic, doesn't it? It's totally possible for you. All you need is a little Shadow Work and new habit-building. Let's dive in!

Which one needs healing?

If you struggle with any of the following…

- Resting (on the reg, not once you burn out)
- Having days where you don't do anything "productive."
- Surrendering to divine will and divine timing.
- Creative expression
- Trust issues
- Control issues
- Receiving money, love, and other forms of abundance
- Going with the flow
- Changing your plan or schedule
- Bashing your partner or the opposite sex (even as a joke)

You have too much masculine energy and need to heal and balance your feminine energy.

If you struggle with any of the following…

- Sticking to a schedule
- Setting boundaries
- Making decisions
- Following through with commitments
- Finishing what you started
- Changing your limiting beliefs
- Watching too much TV
- Spending too much time scrolling through social media
- Expressing your love for your partner (in their love language)

- Feast and famine spending patterns with your money

You have too much feminine energy and need to heal and balance your masculine energy.

It's very common for aspects of both your feminine and masculine energy to need attention and healing.

Another big clue will be to look at your primary relationships with your parents and/or parental figures. These were your main examples of masculine and feminine energy as a child and young adult. Their ways of being were imprinted on you. This informs the masculine and feminine energies you experience and express now. Let's go a little deeper.

Your Mom

What was your relationship like with your mom? What is it like now? Was she a stay-at-home mom, or did she go to work? Did she express her love and affection for you, or did that stop at a certain age? Have you been able to cultivate a healthy friendship with your mom, or are you somewhat estranged?

Did your mom follow her heart and express her creativity in the world? Or did she over-identify with the role of mother and project all her expectations and unfulfilled desires onto you? What's her personality like? Was she able to receive help from others, or did she think she had to do everything herself for it to be done right? Was she kind or abrasive? Did she trust others, or did she need to control them?

These questions are important to ask when going about healing your feminine energy. If you struggle with any of the issues I shared above, there will be something to address.

Write your responses in your journal or workbook.

What was/is your Mom like? What was/is your relationship with her like?

What about what you wrote above could be contributing to your difficulties in expressing or balancing your feminine energy?

Speaking to the Mother

Now that you've explored, I invite you to write a letter to your mom in your journal or workbook. In that letter, I want you to express all the things that you haven't been able to say to her. Express all the things still living within you and causing you any type of pain.

I want you to go there, get nasty, and use foul language; don't hold anything back. Once you finish writing the letter, I want you to read it out loud to yourself. Allow any feelings or emotions to come up and move through you.

I'll help you get started.

Dear Mom,

I've created a quick and powerful guided meditation that will help you solidify the amazing and deep work you're doing. To access the *Speaking to the Mother Meditation*, visit ***www.ciararubin.com/yakbookresources***

Feminine Power UP

Here are some tips to boost your feminine energy:

- Rest. Take a nap. Or at least lay down without your phone for a few minutes. You can even read a book if you need to keep your mind occupied.

- Take on a creative hobby. It could even be a productive one, like cooking or gardening.

- Go on a "no pants diet." Wear dresses and skirts as much as possible. This illustrates that you're open to attracting your desires into your life.

- Surround yourself with reminders to trust in the Divine timing of all things, get a sticker, and set reminders on your phone to help you surrender to the flow of the universe.

- Let your partner take the lead. Don't fight him on every little thing, pick at him, or make fun of him in front of others.

Your Dad

What was your relationship like with your dad? How is it now? Did you have a birth dad that you didn't know very well? Did you have a stepdad? Did you have one dad that you had a strained relationship with? Did your dad physically abandon you? Did your dad emotionally abandon you at any point?

What was your dad himself like? What was his personality like? Was he kind? Did he go for what he really wanted and live up to his potential, or did he settle? Did he struggle with addictions?

These questions are important to ask when going about healing your masculine energy. If you struggle with any of the issues I shared above, there will be something there to address.

Write your responses in your journal or workbook.

What was/is your Dad like? What was/is your relationship with him like?

What about what you wrote above could be contributing to your difficulties in expressing or balancing your masculine energy?

Speaking to the Father

Now that you've explored, I invite you to write a letter to your dad in your journal or workbook. In that letter, I want you to express everything you haven't been able to say to him. All the things that are still living within you and causing you any type of pain.

I want you to go there, get nasty, use foul language, don't hold anything back. Once you finish writing the letter, I want you to read it out loud to yourself. Allow any feelings or emotions to come up and move through you.

I'll help you get started.

Dear Dad,

I've created a quick and powerful guided meditation to solidify the amazing work you're doing. To access the *Speaking to the Father Meditation*, visit ***www.ciararubin.com/yakbookresources***

Masculine Power UP

Here are some tips to boost your masculine energy:

- Create a daily, stupid, easy habit for yourself. It could be a 3-minute meditation. A 5-minute yoga practice. A 2-minute movement or gratitude journaling practice. It doesn't matter what it is, but it needs to be 5 minutes or less and be non-negotiable.

- You need to do it every single day, 7 days a week, for at least 6 months. At the end of the 6 months, you can add to the practice, change it or reevaluate it.

- Set time limits on the social media apps on your phone, and set a time when all the apps on your phone are inaccessible. This could be at a certain time of night until a certain time in the morning. Stick with your social media and phone limits for at least 3 months.

  - If you fall off the wagon, don't beat yourself up. Get right back on the next day. We'll talk a little bit more about this in Step 3.

- Create a budget for your personal finances. Track your spending habits. Make adjustments so that you can meet your larger financial goals.

- If you've committed to a social event or meetup, do not cancel it unless you're sick or an emergency arises. I know you know that most things are not emergencies.

  - Even if you don't feel like going, go anyway. Practice saying No the next time. I'll share more about checking in with your inner Yes and No in Step 4.

Now that you're ready to see yourself fully, it's time for the practical how-to on healing shadows.

Chapter 11:
How to Heal Shadows (in 7 steps)

Though it becomes easier with practice, healing shadows is never easy. Taking a look at yourself and your faults is painful. You are brave and amazing for moving forward with this process. Shadow Work will heal the world; you are part of that legacy. You're changing your life for the better. You'll feel better than you ever imagined you could. You'll start seeing the practical results all around you.

Facing and healing your shadows is not easy, but it can be simple. Over the years, I've become a self-proclaimed Shadow Work junkie. It's still not easy for me to take a look at my faults and the challenges in my life. Yet, part of me looks forward to it because I've developed these shadow-working tools I'm sharing with you. I've done enough Shadow Work to know the freedom and success that comes on the other side of the darkness. Let's go step by step together, starting with Awareness.

Step 1: Awareness

If you're going to heal a shadow, the first step is to become aware of what that shadow even is. This is going to be a surface-level problem or challenge. Use this process to become aware of the negative behavior trait(s) you want to change about yourself or the area of your life you want to improve.

Here are some examples of places to look for shadows:

- A relationship that ended (romantic, friendship)
- A difficult family relationship
- Friendship(s) that feel unfulfilling or draining
- Challenges with your child
- Challenges with your partner
- Traumatic experiences, which can be from childhood on, ranging from:
  - Full-on physical, mental, or emotional trauma
  - Low-key embarrassment or small infractions over years
- Parts of your job that you hate
- People at work that annoy you
- Neighbors who annoy you
- Parts of your business that aren't working (or aren't working as well as they should)
- Any aspect of your life that you regularly struggle with or complain about
- Any aspect of your life that you historically struggle with or complain about

For the purposes of this exercise, I'm going to take you through two examples of shadows I've healed from my own life.

At the end of this book will be a chart that takes you through the 7 steps of Shadow Work without my examples.

Example one: Friendship Breakup

In the past, I was friends with a girl I thought was amazing! She was a go-getter and had her own business. I tried hard to be close to her, and was even at her wedding party (she was in mine too). We loved analyzing other people. We'd often talk about her other friends and people in her life.

Yet, I never felt like she saw me as her equal, and the friendship was always pretty one-sided. I'd be the one to reach out and make plans to spend time together, and I was always cheering her on. She'd often ghost me for weeks at a time, and I'd always be the one to contact her and ask if everything was okay.

At one point, she admitted to me that she wasn't great at being a friend, and I hoped she'd try harder, but she never did. Once I got into spirituality, she ghosted me again. This time, I let her go.

Example two: Romantic Breakup

My high school boyfriend dumped me. We'd been dating for almost 2 years. He went on a 10-day cruise with his family without cell service. The day he came back, I was so excited to see him! He called me on his way over to my house to pick me up for dinner, and on the phone, I could tell things were off.

He told me I didn't fit the picture of the woman he saw himself with long-term. What he saw for his life. That we needed to break up. I felt blindsided and devastated. He came to the door, and I was in a fit of rage and sadness. I threw every piece of jewelry he'd given me at him. He sat on the couch as I wailed in his lap for over an hour. Once I calmed down a bit, he left. I never saw or talked to him again.

Pick one thing from your own life that you want to heal, and write your responses in your journal or workbook.

AWARENESS: What Shadow do you want to heal? Pick the first thing that comes to mind: the low-hanging fruit. Make a list of all the Shadows that come to the forefront of your mind below.

Write the answer to this question in your journal or workbook: How does awareness of this/these shadow(s) make you feel?

Step 2: Intention

Now that you're aware of the shadow, it's time to set your intention. Intentions are a powerful and crucial part of any spiritual and emotional work. Your intentions (whether you're aware of them or not) are paving the way for all manifestations and the reality you experience.

Example one: Friendship Breakup

I want to see my part in this unfulfilling friendship. To become aware of why/how I attracted this friendship in the first place so that I won't do it again.

Example two: Romantic Breakup

I don't want to be angry with him anymore. I want to be free of whatever beliefs and traits I hold on to due to the pain I experienced in that relationship.

INTENTION: So, what do you want? How do you want to feel after healing this shadow? What do you hope shifts in your life as a result of facing this demon? Write your responses in your journal or workbook.

Step 3: The Root

Awareness and intention will pave the way to finding the root of your issue. Awareness was about the surface problem, the effect of your shadow. The cause of the shadow will be different. It's linked to a limiting belief, dysfunctional behavior, and/or traumatic situation.

The limiting beliefs that live in your subconscious are not always immediately obvious. If discovering the root of your shadow takes a few days or even a few weeks, I don't want you to lose heart or give up!

To be honest, how long it takes to become aware of the root is up to you. Do you truly want to heal this shadow? Are you committed to becoming someone you love a lot more? Are you committed to achieving all the success that's possible for you? This comes down to a decision; it's that simple. You get to choose whether you decide to become someone who walks their talk.

Finding the root takes a little exploration. I'll make it easy by applying the triggers exercise we explored earlier.

Below, I'll reiterate my examples. Then, I'll use the trigger exercise to find the shadows connected to them.

Example one: Friendship Breakup

The issue: I was in a one-sided friendship with someone I put on a pedestal. She gossiped about everyone in her life and eventually ghosted me.

Trigger Exploration:

What about this friend triggered or hurt me the most?

1. She talked about all her struggles with her "friends," yet I never felt like she treated me like her best friend. I was clearly the most loyal and thoughtful, but she'd keep me at arm's length.

2. Her ghosting. The way she'd fall off the map and seemingly didn't care whether or not we were friends anymore. How I'd always have to be the one to reach back out to her.

What unhealthy behaviors (of hers) am I seeing within these triggers?

- Gossiping
  - She's talking shit about her friends behind their backs
- Walls up
  - She isn't letting me in or letting herself feel close to me.
- Ghosting
  - Silent treatment and ending the relationship with no gradual boundaries, no warning, and no conversation to explain her wanting to move on.

Oh shit, do I do any of those things, or have I in the past? Yep.

Why do I do those things? I'll focus on the gossiping part.

What is Gossip? Talking shit about someone behind their back. Passing judgment on them because of something I believe they did (due to someone telling me about it). Telling someone else while layering judgment and disdain for their behavior.

My perception is always related to my particular biases, vibrations, experiences, and trauma. So, if I see this person I'm gossiping about in a bad light, it's because of my own perception of them. This doesn't mean that they aren't doing something toxic. My choice to share my judgment with another person is also toxic.

Why is this person triggering me to the point where I gossip about them? Remember the idea I shared about forgiveness: the two reasons you'd feel triggered? So, is this person triggering me because they are exhibiting a trait I haven't empowered myself to yet? Or because they're exhibiting a negative trait I have within myself that I don't like and don't want to face up to?

The understanding of whatever trait of theirs triggered me is gold. From there, I can find the trait within myself. I often used to get triggered when I found out people were talking shit about me behind my back. Which, of course, I was also doing. Now that I gossip a lot less (I'm not saying I'm perfect), I definitely feel less triggered. Less of a need to gossip about them back or "do something about it."

Why do people gossip? I've already explored one reason above: being triggered. As I think more deeply about the moments I've done it, I realize I'm doing it because the other person I'm talking to is doing it. I want to connect with them. It's so strange that we would use something as toxic as gossip to feel connected to one another, but we definitely do.

In today's culture, it seems arrogant not to at least complain about your own life in conversation. The next best thing is to complain about someone else. Bonus points if you're blaming your complaint about your life on someone else and their behavior.

You're co-creating your reality with Spirit. Every experience you have is a manifestation of your higher self. To make you aware of toxic patterns (and also positive patterns). Complaining and blaming someone else for your problems is plainly incorrect. Taking radical personal responsibility for your behaviors and emotions brings true self-empowerment and freedom.

It can be hard to take that perspective. Blaming others and gossiping about them feels easier. However, in the long run, it makes you feel even worse about yourself. It also doesn't solve any of the problems you're having.

With all this exploration, I can take my awareness of the dysfunctional behavior of gossiping and bring it down to the roots:

A desire to connect and feel connected to others. I want to be liked and feel accepted by others. Even if that connection and acceptance require toxic behavior.

If toxic behavior is required to connect with that person, it's not a healthy relationship. If you remove the toxic behavior from the relationship and it dissolves, it's not a worthwhile relationship. If I'm willing to engage in toxic behavior to keep relationships, I have an insecurity. A fear of abandonment. So, to not be abandoned, I've been engaging in toxic behavior.

Now that I've psychoanalyzed myself, I can see that I need to face my fear of abandonment. Take a look at any traumatic experiences in my life that may have led to that fear. This may point me to some significant relationships in my life, both family and romantic. Relationships where I felt abandoned either physically, mentally, emotionally, or all the above.

I hope this example helps you to connect the dots and dig down to the root of your shadow! The next example is a traumatic experience, so it's a little more straightforward.

Example two: Romantic Breakup

The Issue: My high school boyfriend unexpectedly dumped me.

Trigger Exploration:

What about this experience triggered or hurt me the most?

1. The shock and separation. The fact that he'd gone on vacation and I was expecting a fun and beautiful homecoming. If I really think about it, though, there were signs that he wasn't all in before he left.

2. Him telling me that I "didn't fit the picture." This felt demeaning and unfair. Like I wasn't good enough for him, and that was how he rationalized dumping me.

Since this example was a traumatic experience, I'm not going to dive into his dysfunctional behaviors. However, that can also be a valid exploration!

Looking back, I can see that staying in a high school relationship as we embarked on college life wasn't a good idea. He actually did the right thing. But at the time, I was having my own doubts and fears about going off on my own. That relationship was something I was holding onto for comfort. Also, the way he phrased his reasoning. Saying I "didn't fit the picture in his head" made me feel like I wasn't good enough.

So, we have two roots:

1. Fear of abandonment confirmed

   The abandonment wound is deep, and many people have it. Your higher self will manifest situations in your life that reopen old wounds. Then you're forced to pay attention to it and can heal it. I didn't have the maturity or perspective to do so at that time. But once I started my Shadow Work journey, it was an easy place to begin.

   Fearing abandonment can create unhealthy attachments to people and relationships in your life. When you fear abandonment, you might do things that are toxic or out of integrity to maintain relationships. Even if those relationships are unhealthy or have run their course.

2. Limiting Belief: I'm not (good) enough

   This is a limiting belief that can result from abandonment. You've been abandoned because the other person or people couldn't physically or emotionally support you. When you're a child, you tend to believe it's your fault. This isn't a conscious reasoning.

Write your responses in your journal or workbook.

THE ROOT: Use the shadow you're choosing for this exercise to embark on a similar exploration. Discover the root trauma and/or limiting beliefs connected to it.

The Shadow (copy this from your Awareness step):

Trigger Exercise:

What triggered or hurt you most about this?

What unhealthy behaviors (of theirs) are you seeing within these triggers?

Do you do any of those things, or have you in the past? Yep.

Why do you do those things?

The Root(s):

Step 4: Feel It

Now, you've gotten down to the heart of the matter. It's time to let yourself feel all the feelings. This is something that most people avoid. It's safe to get used to allowing yourself to feel these feelings. Your fear and avoidance are much scarier than the process itself.

Your way of avoiding your feelings could come wrapped in the "I'm fine" excuse. This is a common deflection that usually comes from childhood. Your caregivers ignored your big emotions, explained them away, or even shamed them. So I get it; you're "fine," but you're not. You're dissociating and convincing yourself that everything was fine, no big deal. Feelings aren't logical. So even if you can find a very "legitimate" way to logically explain your feelings or why you're "fine," I invite you to trust me. Open up to the idea that there could be value in exploring old feelings.

These feelings could include:

- Confusion
- Anxiety
- Anger
- Disgust
- Frustration
- Terror
- Hatred
- Loathing
- Sadness
- Deep sadness
- Depression

You may have grown up in a household where emotional intelligence wasn't the norm. Or you grew up in a physically, mentally, or emotionally abusive household. Either way, many of these feelings were unsafe to feel and express.

Your adult caregivers didn't know how to handle these feelings themselves. They were never allowed to feel and express these darker, more negative emotions. So, every time you exhibited them, they shut you down, made fun of you, ignored, shamed, or even punished you for acting out. Your caregivers may have been largely unconscious. They were reacting to the outward expression of your negative emotions (your behavior) rather than inquiring about the feelings and motivation behind them.

This isn't your fault, and this was not their fault. Your adult caregivers may be responsible for some (or a lot) of the negative emotion stored within your energy field. Acknowledging that doesn't mean you're blaming them. You have the opportunity to break vicious cycles of emotional weakness.

When I say emotional weakness, I mean the inability to feel and process all your positive and negative emotions in a healthy way. True strength is the ability to feel deeply. To give yourself the space and time to feel all your emotions so that they move through you and don't keep you stuck.

The Physical Release Types

What I'm going to share with you now are the 4 physical release types. Though the energy stuck inside of you is mental or emotional, you're still a physical being. So, to dissolve your shadow, you must experience that release physically. What follows are four techniques you can use by themselves and altogether to "feel it" while facing any shadow.

Journaling

I already see you rolling your eyes. Writing down your feelings is a sure-fire way to bring those feelings back into your conscious awareness. Typing it out on the computer or into a note on your phone just doesn't have the same flavor as pen to paper.

You may have had some kind of trauma related to journaling. An invasion of privacy. Someone shaming you for not being smart enough in your writing. Having something personal that you wrote exploited or made fun of. You don't feel safe expressing your true feelings anywhere that isn't your own mind. Trauma like this may have silenced you. You may have been silenced before in other ways in other lifetimes.

Perhaps you feel that writing out your feelings is too much work. Let's immediately psychoanalyze this: you are not too much work. You and your big feelings are not too much. You deserve and are worthy of having your feelings expressed and seen. Taking proper care of yourself includes caring for your emotional health. You are worthy of being taken care of properly.

You must overcome these ancient gag orders; your voice in writing must be seen and heard by you, at the very least. Witnessing yourself in writing is crucial to healing and transmuting your shadows into light.

I invite you to set a timer for 10 minutes and allow your pen to flow. Even if you're unsure what to write, write that you're not sure what to write, and keep going! I'll give you a prompt at the end of this chapter so that you can explore the shadow you're working on through writing.

Speaking

Saying your feelings out loud is powerful. Sometimes, it can be difficult to say the things you want to say to someone who hurt you in the moment. And so those feelings and words stay stuck in your throat and energy field. I'm not saying you need to confront everyone who's hurt you. Saying your feelings out loud to yourself is often enough to allow the feelings to come all the way to the surface. It'll give you the catharsis you need to let go of the shadow.

Try doing the writing exercise first, and then read your writing out loud to yourself. This is especially helpful if the writing alone didn't make you cry.

One more thing I want to mention under the speaking release type is music. Music is a powerful form of artistic expression that is full of emotion. It can help you get in touch with your deeper, shadowy emotions. I've been using music and singing to release shadow since I was around 9 or 10. Of course, I had no idea I was doing "Shadow Work" back then!

All you have to do is reflect on a song that makes you feel the way the shadow you're facing makes you feel. Maybe there's a song that helps you express anger, like *Fighter* by Christina Aguilera. Or maybe there's a song that speaks to the depths of your sadness, like *Almost Lover* by A Fine Frenzy.

You don't have to be a singer for this to work. In fact, YOUR voice singing along to a song that makes you feel something is the most effective tool. Rather than listening to someone else sing. So:

- Find your song

- Play it in a place where you can be alone for about 10 to 15 minutes

- Sing along with it while reflecting on the feelings brought up by the shadow you're facing.

- Allow all feelings to come to the surface with patience and compassion for yourself.

Sweating

It might sound kind of funny, but releasing stuck feelings through sweat is totally a thing. We know by now that water holds emotion. There are a few different ways you can do this. You can set the intention to release your feelings before you go into a sauna. Or before an exercise session. You can imagine the feelings and limiting beliefs pouring off of you through your sweat.

Another point I want to include in this physical release type is sex. You may or may not sweat while you have sex, but sex is a powerful way to intend and release stuck feelings. More specifically, orgasm is an extremely effective way to heal yourself. So when I say sex, it could be with a partner you love and trust or with yourself.

Using sex to heal yourself will not work with a casual partner or someone you don't trust. So, if you want to use your sexuality and orgasm to heal, and you're not in a loving partnership, I recommend cultivating a self-pleasure practice. Kim Anami is one of my favorite teachers on this topic.

Crying

I've saved the best for last. All the other physical release types can, and SHOULD, lead to this one: crying. Crying is the fastest and most permanent way to release shadow and limiting beliefs. It ensures that you feel any lingering negative emotions. That you're truly healing from any trauma you've experienced. When you cry, your body literally vibrates. On an energetic level, your body is moving stuck energy up and out of your aura and being.

The trouble is you might not feel comfortable with crying. So many messages from our culture, society, and caregivers say crying is unacceptable. "I'll give you something to cry about!" "Don't cry, please don't cry!" "There's no crying in baseball."

There's so much fear of crying. It's interesting because you often fear the thing you need most or need to face the most. Crying is one of the healthiest things a human can do, whether crying tears of joy or sorrow. Expressing the full extent of your emotions is more powerful than you know.

Emotional mastery is something uniquely human. To achieve that mastery, you need to be a master at crying your freaking eyes out. It's funny because you fear the tears. You try to hold them back as much as you can. Yet, in those few moments when you finally do let yourself break down, I know that there's a part of you that feels good. It always feels damn good after a good cry.

If you have trouble getting to a place where you can cry during your Shadow Work process, use the above physical release types first.

- Journaling your feelings is a good way to start to get back in touch with those forbidden feelings.

- Then, you can read your writing aloud. Or simply speak aloud the things you've always wanted to say.

- Then, you can play a song you feel relates to how you feel about the situation and sing along.

- You could even go for a run or walk while reflecting on the situation. The movement of your body could allow the tears to come.

Crying is crucial to letting go of your traumas in a way that stops them from continuing to manifest. Even if they do, you're no longer beholden to or triggered by those things because you've truly let them go. Once you allow yourself to cry, your shadow no longer has power over you.

Example one: Friendship Breakup

Gossiping/Desperation to connect/Fear of abandonment

For this shadow, some journaling sessions and singing songs that felt aligned were enough to make me cry and feel the hurts I'd been avoiding. I've done this on more than one occasion for just this friendship. Sometimes, she still shows up in my dreams. When she does, I know it's time for another FEEL IT session.

Example two: Romantic Breakup

Painful Breakup/Abandonment/Belief of not being "enough"

I've written several letters to my ex-boyfriend. Detailing all my feelings about our relationship and the break-up. I've read these letters aloud to myself. I've brought about tears in several "breakdown" sessions. I've also found a few songs that make me think about this person and what happened in our relationship. I sing these songs to myself when I have time alone, usually in the shower, and bring more tears that way.

One way to know if you have healed your shadows around a specific person is if they continue to show up in your dreams. This particular ex-boyfriend used to show up in my dreams a lot more. He still does every now and again, but significantly less than before, maybe once or twice a year. That's saying something! I dream vividly and in detail every single night.

FEEL IT PRACTICE

In the space your journal or workbook, free write about the Shadow you're currently facing. Write at the top of the page: "What do I need to remember and feel about (insert your situation/trauma/behavior/root?)."

Then, set a timer for 10 minutes and write non-stop. If you're not sure what to write, write "I'm not sure what to write," and keep going until the timer stops. Let it all out in the confidence that no one else will ever see this (you can even burn it afterward to make sure). Don't try to be proper or polite. Dig deep.

Now, read your writing aloud. If there are any emotions or tears that come up, stop reading for a moment. Allow yourself to cry until you feel the crying come to a stopping point. Then, continue until you've read the entire piece.

If you still haven't cried, or if you feel there's more emotion, reflect on a song that relates to what you're facing. Go with the first song that pops into your head. Listen to the song, sing along, and allow yourself to feel the feels and cry.

Feel free (see what I did there?) to try any of the other release types I mentioned above.

Step 5: Let the Light IN

Now you've done the gnarly work of feeling your feelings. You've had a catharsis. It's time for the very important step of letting the light in. When you release stuck energy, emotion, and shadow, you create a void within your energy field. The universe always fills a void. So, immediately after clearing space within your energy field, you must intend, imagine, and allow light to fill that void.

This is the step that sounds the most "woo woo," but I can tell you it does absolutely make a difference.

BUT: I don't want to make the mistake of telling you that you'll never be tested by this shadow again. It's highly likely that you've had other experiences in your life that have pressed on this wound and added to this shadow. All core wounds will continue to be tested. But the more you face these issues, the less triggered you'll be each time the Universe tests you with a similar situation.

Remember: when you clear shadow energy, you're taking off pairs of goggles and seeing the world more clearly. This means that if you ever encounter a person or situation again that triggers this same shadow, you'll recognize it for what it is. You'll realize that you have the power to choose how you react to it. Instead of feeling powerless and victimized by it.

LET THE LIGHT IN PRACTICE

Put on a five-minute meditation track or song that lights you up on the inside. Sit down with your eyes closed. Imagine light pouring into the space you've created with your catharsis. Extra points if you do this meditation while sitting outside in the sun.

Guided meditation recorded on *www.ciararubin.com/yakbookresources*.

Step 6: Intention 2.0

Reflect on your Intention from Step 2, and adjust it now that you're seeing things more clearly. Create your new belief.

Here are mine:

Example one: Friendship Breakup

I want to feel like I'm the good person I claim to be. I want people to see me as a person with integrity, someone who's trustworthy and kind.

New Belief: I am trustworthy, kind, and full of integrity. I am a good person.

Example two: Romantic Breakup

I don't want to be angry with him anymore. I want to be free of whatever beliefs and traits I hold on to due to the pain I experienced in that relationship.

New belief: I am good enough. I am loved. I allow myself to feel and release my anger in healthy ways.

Turn your new beliefs into affirmations that you put into reminders on your phone. Write them onto note cards that you place in conspicuous places around your home. Say these new beliefs out loud to yourself throughout the day as you see them.

Rewrite your intentions in your journal or workbook. from Step 2 below, and turn them into affirmations.

Intention:

New Belief:

Say your affirmations out loud to yourself 3 times. Bonus points if you put them in your phone, write them down, and put them up around your home.

Step 7: Habit Time

There are some new habits that you need to develop to make the healing permanent. To move your life in that area on an upward trajectory.

For now, a simple awareness of the new habit(s) you want/ need to cultivate and writing them down is important.

That could also involve breaking yourself of a bad habit. Healing the shadow associated with that habit will take you far in terms of awareness. Yet, you still may find yourself in situations where the old habit is triggered. For all things habit-breaking and building, I recommend the book *Atomic Habits* by James Clear.

For the purposes of this exercise, I'll give you my examples and then give you space to choose new habits.

Example one: Friendship Breakup

Habit to break: Gossiping! No more spreading hearsay information or private information of other people. It's okay to share about situations you're going through. It's not okay to share drama or a victim mentality perspective.

Once I realized the root of why I was gossiping, I was able to observe myself in social situations. Now, when I notice someone else gossiping, I try to listen without adding anything to it. Or I'll say something compassionate about the person they're gossiping about. This usually nips the situation in the bud, and the other person moves on to another topic.

I continue to observe myself during conversations. I do my best to curb any old inclination to gossip or share "breaking news" about someone else.

Habits to build:

- Staying quiet.

- Excusing myself from a conversation that starts to go in the direction of gossip

- Redirecting the conversation

- Calling myself out for gossiping in the moment

Example two: Romantic Breakup

Habit to break: Blaming my ex-boyfriend for anything. Including any residual behavior or dysfunction. I also need to break the habit of feeling like I'm not good enough.

Habit to build: Take radical personal responsibility for my thoughts, emotions, and behavior. Reflect on things that contribute to those negative thoughts, emotions, and behavior without blaming others.

I also need to build a habit that makes me feel worthy and good enough for my time and attention. This could be a new self-care habit. Improving an area of my life to show myself that I am worthy. That I don't need someone else to validate that worthiness.

HABIT TIME: Your turn in your journal or workbook please write!

Habit to break:

Habit to build:

Shadow Healed, For Now

I want to congratulate you for your courageous work in healing this shadow. It's no small thing, believe me. So many people avoid this work and live inauthentic lives.

If you're an entrepreneur or want to be, healing your shadows is everything for your business. Your business is always a reflection of you and your vibration. If something is going wrong in your business, it's a direct result of something going wrong in your life.

That said, it's time to move forward with your new understanding and habits. Eventually, you'll encounter another shadow. When I first started Shadow Work, I thought that once I healed a particular shadow or limiting belief, I could wash my hands of it.

It's true that as I healed the shadow, my beliefs would become less limiting, and my habits would become more self-honoring and loving. But I still find that the shadows return (in a different way) to test me. Shadow Work is cyclical, and you came into this life with your unique yet universally human set of shadows and demons to face. Every time you face one of them, you become stronger and gain the tools to dig deeper and heal on an even deeper level.

Spiritual Bypassing

Spiritual bypassing is the practice of:

- Avoiding
- Ignoring
- Or intellectualizing

shadows and traumas without actually processing them. Many spiritual seekers and even teachers become addicted to the process of expansion. Learning new knowledge that expands your Consciousness is fun, exciting, and feels great! Yet, expansion without integration or healing becomes unbalanced righteousness.

Sometimes, it feels easier to leave a shadow alone. The feelings and behaviors it creates are comfortable and familiar. Even if the effects of the shadow are negative, you may experience resistance to looking at it or healing it. Sometimes, the "devil you know" feels better than the unknown.

In the short term, embracing the concepts of "love and light" might feel better without any emotional processing. But in the long term, the shadow will still be rumbling beneath all your crystals, sage, and mantras. No amount of "spiritual stuff" or spiritual events you attend will erase or replace your need for Shadow Work.

Spiritual bypassing is becoming a thing of the past. Shadow Work is becoming normalized, thank goodness! But be aware of those in your circles who seem like something is off. Be aware of spiritual teachers and leaders who feel out of balance. They may be wise and charismatic, yet you can sense something is off with their energy. Spiritual bypassing is usually the culprit.

I want to reiterate that I understand that Shadow Work is uncomfortable. It's a process of intentionally becoming uncomfortable. Intentionally taking a look at things you don't like about yourself. Being honest about the events or people connected to those things. Oftentimes, fear of looking into the darkness becomes all-consuming. Most people avoid it like the plague. Taking a look at your shadows is not as scary as your logical mind is making it seem.

Once you're in the muck, armed with the tools I'm giving you, you'll find that you're braver than you thought you were. That you're much stronger than you know. And with Spirit, God, your higher self, and your guides by your side, there is nothing you cannot face.

Now you know the step-by-step on how to heal shadows! Let's have a little fun and talk about using your dreams to help you heal your shadows.

Chapter 12:
Dreamwork for Shadow Work

Whether or not you remember your dreams, I assure you that you dream every single night. When your consciousness leaves your body after you fall asleep, it heads into the astral realms, and you have a dream experience.

Because of this, you have a front-row seat for what's going on in your subconscious. The parts of you that you're not always aware of. That's why your dreams are such a valuable tool in Shadow Work. Because they show you the truths that you may not be able to conclude on your own with your mind while you're awake.

If you'd like to add this powerful tool to your shadow work toolbox, I'll teach you how to use it! The quick and dirty, step-by-step version, of course. ;)

But first, What Actually Are Dreams?

You leave your body every night and head to the astral realms. There are many ways to explore these astral realms. To develop your intuition and do Shadow Work, your dreams are a window into your subconscious.

You must understand the depth of symbolism, metaphor, and even literal information held within your dreams. The spiritual and non-physical realms make up the majority of the universe. Your physical body and material experience only make up a small percentage of reality.

With this understanding, you can conclude that your dreams are almost more true, or at least more honest than your waking life. The more Shadow Work you do, and the more you understand your dreams, this will start to shift. You'll start to live more true to who you are in your waking life. You'll use your dreams to assess what's going on in your subconscious.

Your subconscious is all the parts of your operating system that you're not fully aware of. The parts of you "in shadow" that still have the power to call the shots and co-create your reality. These are the memories and experiences that you don't consciously remember. These are your beliefs, both limiting and supportive. Once you become aware of an aspect of your subconscious, you become conscious. When you're conscious, you have more control over what you're manifesting into your reality.

It's valuable to remember your dreams and take them seriously as clues for what's going on with you. Dreams are a function of your clairvoyance. So that means that they're metaphorical, symbolic, and sometimes literal. I'm definitely not saying to take your dreams as prophecy, though some dreams may be.

We're going to operate on the premise that all your dreams are symbolic. Your dreams are your higher self trying to give you a leg up. Showing you exactly what your problems are, the things that are holding you back.

Because your dreams are so blunt at times, it can be tough to accept responsibility for what you're seeing. It can be very easy and even seductive to feel like you're a victim in your dreams. I assure you that you are co-creating your entire dream. That everyone and everything that you encounter in your dreams is another aspect of you.

Your dreams are you exploring yourself. No one is coming to harm you. It's only you who is attacking yourself by creating a reality in which you feel attacked. We'll dive more into this concept in Step 3 of the book. For now, understand that your dreams are all about you and your true feelings about people and things.

How to Recall Your Dreams (in 4 steps)

1. Intention

The first step in recalling your dreams is the easiest one: setting the intention before you go to sleep. Before you go to sleep, write yourself a reminder on a sticky note that you leave by your bed where you can see it. Set your intention to have a meaningful dream and remember it when you wake up.

So, it's a two-step intention.

- Step one is to set the intention to have a meaningful dream. To give you insight on what you're going through right now. Or generally, to let you know what's going on with you.

- Step two is to set the intention to actually remember the dream when you wake up. We often have long and involved dreams, and immediately upon waking up, they slip away. Step two will help you hold on to your dream.

2. Record

It's important to record the dream as close to immediately upon waking as you can. You can keep a journal beside your bed to jot down a few bullet points you remember. This will help you flesh out the dream once you're more awake and can fill in the blanks.

You can also record a voice note immediately upon waking. Get into the habit of running through the major bullet points of your dream in your head before you wake up. This will help you find themes, symbols, and patterns that you can apply meaning to and use to get your answers. Once you've recorded your dream, it's time for review.

3. Review

Review the bullet points you've written down or the voice note you've recorded on your phone. Add any details you remember as you jog your memory with bullet points. You may already start seeing some patterns or themes popping out. In this step, it's important to write down any common symbols that you could use to apply meaning to. I'll give you some ideas on common symbols once we get through step four, which is to develop your dream symbols.

4. YOUR Symbols

This is super important! Your dream symbols will relate to your life and how you understand the world. Spirit will always speak your language so that you can easily understand. What this means is:

- Whatever your interests are

- Whatever pop culture references you enjoy or resonate with

- Whatever music or movie themes or artists or actors you are familiar with

Will be the things that appear in your dreams.

This also includes favorite colors or animals. It's important to develop your own dream symbols. That way, you can accurately assess what is happening in your dream and what it means. Dream symbol books are useful when you're first starting out. But you have to remember that the symbols in those books are the dream symbols of the person who wrote the book. They may have different interests, pop culture references, and ways in which they understand the world. Their dream symbols may not be totally accurate for you, your dreams, and your life.

You'll start to see common symbols repeating and showing up for you. Now, I'll share some common dream symbols that you can look out for and begin to make your own meaning for them.

Common Dream Symbols

Colors

All colors have a psychological and emotional meaning. Many times, when you're first starting to recall your dreams, colors are easy to remember. You can set the intention to remember the most important color before falling asleep. Colors do have psychological meanings, and they also correspond with the chakras.

Here are the chakra colors:

<u>Chakra</u>	<u>Color</u>
Root	Red
Sacral	Orange
Solar Plexus	Yellow
Heart	Green
Throat	Light Blue
Third Eye	Indigo
Crown	Violet

It would be helpful to write down in your dream journal all the colors of the rainbow, as well as brown, black, and white. Then, write your associated meaning with those colors.

Feelings

This one will definitely come up in your dreams, especially if you're clairsentient. Sometimes, feelings will be the only part of a dream you remember. Pay attention to the feelings you experience in the dream. Notice the overall feeling you had in the dream. These feelings will point to clues that tell you what's going on in your subconscious and what could be blocking you.

Animals

Animals are an important part of our human life, so of course, they're going to show up in your dreams. Some people, like me, are into spirit animals and animal totems. So, if you ever have an animal show up in your dream, look up what that animal means spiritually and symbolically. This will give you more answers and ways to apply meaning to your dream.

People

This one has layers and is also very important. There will always be people in your dreams. It's important to notice which people show up in your dreams. Also, what feelings you may associate with those people. It could be people that you know or knew in the past. They could represent the person they're showing up as or an aspect of you. Traits or limiting beliefs you've taken on due to your relationship with them. Write down any people you recognize in your dream and what those people mean to you. This will give you huge insight.

Places

The places you encounter (or are in) during your dream are another important symbol. Often, the places we encounter in our dreams are made-up places that are an amalgamation of:

- Places you've been

- Places you've seen in movies

- Even places you wish you could go.

Think of the place you're in during your dream as the "container" for the dream. What are your surroundings? Are they cluttered or clear? Are you inside or outside? Are you in your childhood home or a haunted house? The location of your dream is significant and will help you apply meaning.

5. Apply Meaning

You'll be able to use the information you're gathering to apply meaning to your day-to-day life. A lot of people second-guess themselves when it comes to applying meaning to their dreams. Move forward confidently with the understanding that you are developing your intuition. It's getting stronger every day, and that deep down, you always know:

- What's going on with you

- What's best for you

- How to move forward

Even if it scares you. What do the symbols you've gathered mean to you? What comes up for you when you think about the colors, feelings, animals, people, and places? Write down the first thing that comes to mind.

Dream Initiation

I'm going to share a dream experience I had years ago that ended up being more of an initiation. I was living in my house on a pond at the time, and as I entered the dream space, I noticed I was in my house.

Whenever you're dreaming where you fell asleep, it's more of an in-between state. An experience mixed with the dream dimension. I noticed that I was in my kitchen, crouched behind the island. I was peering out the French doors, watching a group of about 5-7 people approach the house. I tried to stay out of sight, hoping they wouldn't see me.

They came right up to the door, cupping their hands around their eyes so they could see inside. They immediately spotted me. They motioned for me to come over, so I got up and opened the door, letting them inside. One man and woman seemed to be the leaders of the group, and also a couple. He had dark hair and was wearing black clothes and a leather jacket. She had blonde hair.

The entire group let themselves into my home. They nonchalantly placed a large trunk on the floor in my dining room. The leader of the group unlocked the trunk with the key. The group members began taking all the items out of the trunk and setting them up on the floor. First, there was a long rug. They placed candles, crystals, bones, and feathers on the rug. The leader's girlfriend took an old, worn deck of tarot cards out of her breast pocket and handed them to the leader.

He motioned us to sit down along the rug and around the objects. I reluctantly sat down amongst them. The leader began to walk around us, saying words in a strange language. As he spoke and walked, he was pulling cards from the deck and flicking them onto the rug in front of us. The cards seemed to come alive, and each time he'd flick a new card, blood would fly from it and into our faces.

I soon saw this was a dark magic ritual and wanted no part of it. I realized that I was dreaming, and in my lucid state, I stood up and indignantly walked toward the stairs. I saw the light switch and knew what I had to do. I flipped it up and stated loudly and clearly that I was for the light. That I have always been for the light and always will be for the light. As I began to walk up the stairs, the objects, the rug, the trunk, and the people began to disappear.

I woke up astounded at what I'd experienced. You may have scary dreams like this, or even apocalyptic or disaster dreams. As you continue to do your Shadow work and develop your dream abilities, these types of dreams will start to go away. You can always become lucid and claim your sovereignty and allegiance to all that is light and love.

Come Through!

I hope you've enjoyed this part of the book, where we explored the ideas of Shadow Work and Dream Work. I want to restate that shadow work is the most important part of developing and trusting your intuition.

Clearing shadows, busting through limiting beliefs, and healing your trauma is the only permanent and full-of-integrity way to develop your intuition to the point where it's accurate.

Where you're no longer projecting your issues onto other people but rather are seeing the truth and the heart of the matter.

This is a practice that I encourage you to make part of your lifestyle. Shadow Work is a lifestyle that helps you love yourself and get out of your own way. Shadow Work also makes you and your intuition increasingly sensitive. This sensitivity is powerful. It will help you make decisions with confidence and certainty from your intuition. This sensitivity deserves a spiritual level of self-care.

In the next part of the book, we will dive deep into spiritual self-care. That way, you can take proper care of yourself and your intuition. We'll begin with the practical aspects of spiritual self-care. Then, we'll delve into the crucial spiritual self-care mindset.

STEP 3:
Spiritual Self-Care

Chapter 13:
A New, True Me

This is when I get real with you about what can happen to your relationships as you develop your intuition. I feel like I should be writing this book from a "marketing position." Giving you all the easy buttons and hacks to develop and trust your intuition.

I wish that this journey could have been a lot easier for me. Because I'm sharing everything I've learned so far, I know it will be at least a little easier for you. But that doesn't mean it is easy. It's important that you get used to doing hard things. Doing hard things will become easier. You'll get more comfortable with being uncomfortable.

Changing the trajectory of your life isn't easy. Marital bliss, life purpose fulfillment, and financial wealth aren't things you can hack. If someone says they can, beware. When I tell you that part of this journey is losing the relationships holding you back, I say that from deep personal experience.

Maybe the people in your life right now have great boundaries. They respect your boundaries, inspire you, and love and celebrate you for all of who you are. Or maybe you have a few people like that in your life, but many of the people surrounding you are more attached to the old version of yourself. The people around you are comfortable with your semi-people-pleasing ways. When you start to take better care of yourself, it'll rock their worlds. You'll be illustrating to them the ways in which they're not taking good care of themselves.

I very much believe in the saying that we are the sum of the five people we spend the most time with. So, if the people you spend the most time with aren't living the life of your dreams, it's time for a reality check. My reality check came hard and fast after diving into Shadow Work and spiritual self-care. The more shadows I healed, the more I stopped the dysfunctional behaviors that bonded me to my friends. Things like gossip, watching reality TV and horror movies, eating terrible food, and drinking to the point of blackout.

The sharper my intuition became, the more I started to see that many of the friendships in my life were one-sided. Some of them were "performative" friendships. Where we were both doing the typical things that you would want an ideal best friend to do. Just so that we could say that we had a best friend.

When I started to become aware of the shadow sides of these friendships, I realized that they didn't have much substance. The more I healed and empowered myself, the more awkward it got to hang out with them. They didn't want to talk about anything real. They were annoyed and concerned when I'd bring up chakras, spirit animals, or angel numbers. Some considered themselves to be Christians. But once I started talking about my personal relationship with Jesus, where I was talking to him and could hear him talking back, it weirded them out.

I'm not a Christian, but I do love Jesus. His teachings have massive value for the world at large and for individuals. You don't need to be a Christian to love Jesus, and you don't need to be a "New Ager" to develop and trust your intuition. Your intuition is a part of your human experience that isn't tapped into yet. Your extra senses that are available to you because you're a living, breathing human being.

Once I started being myself and stopped gossiping, there wasn't a whole lot to talk about. Admittedly, I was a little overzealous about the spiritual topics I was learning because it was all new to me.

They wanted the old Ciara. The one who was a lot more spooky and edgy. Now I was over here talking about loving yourself, eating kale, and meditating. From their perspective, I was a square. Though to me, life was magical for the first time, in the most real way. They thought I was crazy. Even telling my husband as such behind my back. But I felt like, for the first time in my life, I was actually becoming sane.

It was painful to know that the people I'd invested so much time, love, and energy into weren't on board with this newer, more true version of me. But it wasn't their fault. I wasn't the friend they'd signed up for. They'd never signed up for spirituality or personal development. These were my choices. They were the right choices for me, but that doesn't mean that my friends also had to go on this journey.

I wish they had, but I sure as hell wouldn't let them hold me back from the deep satisfaction I'd gained in knowing who I am. So I let them go. Honestly, it was my entire bridal party other than my sibling and cousin, with whom I've since lost touch or cut ties. But losing friends wasn't the hardest part. It was facing the end of my marriage.

Before I attended that first Psychic Fair and started on this journey, I was one person. The person who survived my childhood, teenage years, and college experience. Due to the nature of society and growing up with unconscious parents, I felt broken. I've been through many traumatic events, both large and small. I'd developed the dysfunctional behaviors or shadows I talked a little bit about in part two of this book.

I had superficial identity associations. This means I associated my identity with things that didn't have much substance, like pop culture, celebrity culture, and my likes and dislikes. Starting my spiritual journey changed the identity associations I had. I started to pull away from interests, hobbies, and ways of being that I'd held to my whole life.

At my core, I was still the same person. A person who went from broken to satisfied. In the understanding that who I am and what we are as human beings is so much more than we've been told and sold.

All that to say, I was one person when I married my husband. He fell in love with the core of who I am, yes, but also the woman who loved scary movies, gossiping, drinking, and junk food. So, it's fair to say that I became a completely different woman than the woman he married.

I started setting boundaries instead of managing other people's emotions. I started taking better care of myself. Investing in better body products and insisting on a higher quality of food. It raised our household budget a considerable amount.

Also, as I started to love myself more, it became clear all the ways in which my husband didn't love himself. I remember getting into arguments and refusing to raise my voice. I wouldn't take on the emotional anxiety and angst of the conversation. It pissed him off. It was a lot harder to rattle me and bring me into the storm of a useless argument. I admit I wasn't perfect by any measure.

I am, by nature, hard on myself, and I'm working on that. So, at that time, I was also hard on him. I'd started the practice of constantly taking a look at my shadows, so I was constantly calling him out on his shadows as well. Every time he'd resist a new change of mine, I'd push through anyway. I was no longer willing to take part in a lot of the activities that he and I used to enjoy together. My interests were changing, and I could see that a lot of those activities were no longer serving me and my true self. I was very critical of myself and him, and I felt he didn't understand me.

The more my intuition developed, the more spiritually skilled I became, and the more I saw that our marriage could end. From his perspective, I'm sure it was terrifying. The woman he loved was becoming a completely different person in his eyes. Someone he wasn't sure he was in love with. Someone different from the woman he'd spoken beautiful vows to at the altar a year prior.

Also, I was telling him all the ways he was being unconscious on the daily, so I'm sure that was super annoying. We fought constantly. I judged him for his unconscious perspectives and practices. Funny, because I'd been participating in a lot of those perspectives and practices not long before.

The culmination of our struggle came in the form of an ultimatum. I'd had enough of the fighting and was starting to feel stifled by the life I'd created. I'd always dreamed of moving back to California, where I'm from. After the prompting of my spiritual guides, I decided I was going to go for it.

One night, while we were on the way to Chipotle for dinner, I told my husband I'd made a decision: I was going to be moving to California within the next year and that I hoped he'd come with me. I made it very clear that I'd be going whether he came with me or not. Though it was frightening to make such a bold statement that I knew I'd have to back it up with action, I was determined.

He was shocked. I don't think he believed me at first. But over the next two days, he raged and realized that I was for real going to leave him if he didn't come with me. Those two days were some of the hardest I'd ever experienced in my life. I was employing all my spiritual self-care practices like crazy. I needed to hear my intuition and Spirit guides telling me to hold strong and that I was doing the right thing.

Finally, after two days of hell, he told me he'd go with me. That he didn't want to become a starter marriage statistic and that he wanted to give us another shot. His condition was that we make an adventure out of it. Not just to move across the country but to travel by RV and stay in places all over California so that we could decide which area we liked best.

I don't know how I would have made it through those two days without all my spiritual self-care practices. Caving would have been easy. Then I would've stayed stuck.

But in a way, I knew the direction I was moving was more successful and self-empowering than where I'd been. I knew I was loving myself more than I ever had. I was feeling a sense of purpose more than I ever had. I knew I was part of something bigger than myself in my spiritual journey and career. I wouldn't let a relationship get in the way of that.

I'd spent all my teenage years in relationships. Allowing those relationships to take priority over me, my desires, and my truth. Even though this man was the greatest love of my life so far, for the first time, I started to choose myself. It felt hella selfish, uncomfortable, and unfamiliar, illogical even. But my intuition kept guiding me forward and encouraging me to do the right thing.

It can be hard to choose yourself when you fear abandonment. When you've developed your worthiness based on the validation of other people. It can be hard to choose yourself when those choices cause pain to people around you. Yet I want to encourage you and invite you to do it anyway. Even if it means you might lose friends, even if it means your marriage might fall apart.

Do not live the rest of your life stunting your growth and shunning your light for the sake of other people. You may have tons of relationships, but they'll all be built on a lie. Living a life led by your intuition is a life of bravery. Sometimes, it's a life of letting go of the people who aren't meant to be on your journey.

The people who are not willing to do the hard work of creating the momentum toward more success in their lives.

You are worthy of success in your own right. You are worthy of knowing who you are on a deep level and loving that person in a real way. You are worthy. And, who knows, some of those relationships may come along and stay with you in their own way.

Spoiler alert: My marriage did not end. Eight years later, my husband and I are more in love than ever. We're catalysts for each other's growth. We have the best sex we've ever had. We have two beautiful children who were born at home. And we run successful businesses together. If I hadn't trusted my intuition and created all that struggle and discord in our marriage, we wouldn't be where we are today.

I can't take all the credit. My husband very well could have chosen to dig his heels in and divorce me, like several people suggested he do. But he chose a path toward self-love. He chose a path toward self-empowerment and freedom; I'm so glad he did.

My intuition has empowered me to make decisions that feel risky and yet will move me in the right direction—to where I want to be in life and in my business.

As you start to heal your shadows, you and your intuition will become increasingly sensitive and powerful. Your body will become sensitive to harsh chemicals, toxins, foods, and practices that may have been fine for you before. You're stepping into the truth of who you are. Your intuition is becoming loud and accurate. The level of care that you'll need is different.

I don't want to freak you out and make you think you need to adopt all these practices all at once. Stack your habits one at a time, and make them stupid easy. Start with a non-negotiable 3-minute daily habit, and build from there.

First, I'll share the spiritual self-care practices I've developed over the years. Then, I'll give you a crucial spiritual self-care mindset to unlock true safety and self-empowerment.

Chapter 14:
Spiritual Self-care Practices

Salt Soap

Salt is cleansing and purifying both for your physical and energetic bodies. As a sensitive empath, you'll need regular cleansing for your energy. So many empaths take on the energy of other people. They're anxious or depressed when they're actually feeling the anxiety and depression of other people.

Using salt soap on a regular basis will help to clear you of other people's energy. Then you can tell the difference between what's going on with you and what you've taken on from other people. My fave is pink Himalayan salt soap. You can find it on Etsy, Amazon, or wherever you like to shop for your favorite body products.

A few recommendations:

- Ensure you're purchasing a soap with no added artificial fragrances. Artificial fragrance is now known to be as toxic as second hand smoke.

- Salt can dry the skin, so make sure you moisturize after using salt soap.

How To

This is one of the easiest spiritual self-care practices. You can do it while you're already taking your regular shower! About once a week, or whenever you're feeling super drained or overwhelmed with life:

- Wash your body all over with your salt soap.

- Watch the suds rinse off

- Imagine all the negative energy, anxiety, and overwhelm is running off of your body and down the drain

Sage Clearing

Indigenous people have used Sage and Palo Santo for thousands of years. They knew it clears the energy of spaces and people. By using these practices, you're honoring what these beautiful cultures knew to be true about the energetic Universe.

Get some dried Sage or Palo Santo that's been ethically sourced. Use the smoke to clear the energy wherever you feel or think it's heavy. Some people prefer sage, and some prefer Palo Santo. Both of these beautiful plants have a different and unique smell. If you're new to all this, I'd try both of them to see which one you prefer. If you're already familiar with it, here's your sign that your space needs some clearing!

How To

Grab your Sage or Palo Santo and set your intention for the space or the energy you want to clear. This could be your home or a specific room or spot in your home. It could be that you don't have time to take a salt soap shower, and you need to do a quick cleansing of your energy.

- Light your Sage or Palo Santo

- Allow the smoke to fill the space as you walk around, or move the sage up and down your body.

- Imagine the smoke intertwining with the negative energy and removing it.

Don't forget to put your Sage or Palo Santo out before you leave it. Don't be a weirdo and insist on saging other people unless they ask for it or invite you to do it.

Meditation (all types)

You might already be rolling your eyes on the inside reading the word meditation, and I totally get it. Trying to go from your busy life with your busy mind to not thinking about anything is almost impossible. There are so many different types of meditation. If you struggle with "traditional" meditation, don't let that keep you from exploring the practice at all.

Meditation has been huge for me in managing anxiety and connecting to myself, my intuition, and my spirit guides. A few types of meditation I love are movement meditation, music meditation, and mantra. Guided meditations are also a great tool and way to get yourself into the habit of meditating.

As your intuition becomes sharper, meditation becomes a crucial practice to maintain balance and a sense of calm and ease. My meditation practice is what makes me yell at my husband and kids a lot less. I still yell from time to time because I'm still a healing human. Meditation helps me maintain my center when I'm around extended family members who challenge my inner peace.

How To

Movement Meditation

All you have to do is move! You could go for a walk, a run, dance in your living room, workout at the gym, or hike a mountain trail; it doesn't matter. Getting your body moving makes it a lot easier for your mind to stay clear and focused in the moment.

Music Meditation

This is best done to a song with lyrics that you know the words to, one that gives you your desired feeling. If you want to get in touch with your shadows or let out some stuck emotions, play something that gives you the feels and sing along. If you want to clear your mind, play something peaceful and uplifting. If you want to energize, play something sassy. If you're uncomfortable singing in front of people, you may want to do this in your car or the shower.

Guided Meditation

This is an easy one. Find a meditation app you like on your phone. I recommend Insight Timer! Start doing 3-minute guided meditations per day with a teacher you resonate with. Work your way up to a 10-minute daily meditation, and you're ready to begin the mantra meditation.

For guided meditations designed specifically to heal anxiety, frustration, and any other shadows that have been coming up for you as you read this book, visit www.ciararubin.com/ yakbookresources

Mantra Meditation

Chanting Mantras is a great way to put your mind at ease. You can get into an almost trance-like state where you can very easily sense your intuition. This is the first step on the path toward silent meditation. Choose a phrase that's meaningful, motivating, or powerful to you. It could be in your native language, or it could be in an ancient language.

Take some deep breaths and sit cross-legged with your back in proper alignment. Close your eyes and see the phrase inside of your mind's eye. Speak the phrase out loud in a soft voice. Imagine it written over and over again with different colors and materials. You can do this for as little as 2 minutes a day to start off with. Work your way up to at least 10 minutes per day.

Silent Mantra Meditation

This is the exact same thing as the Mantra meditation. Instead of speaking the mantra out loud, you only say it inside your head. Practice the same visualization of the word written in your mind. Start with 2 minutes per day, working your way up to 10 to 15 minutes per day. The first thing in the morning is always the best. But habit-stack it with your other habits and fit it where you can.

Reminder: I've created a TON of guided meditations for you to increase the effectiveness of this book. Go check them out at www.ciararubin.com/yakbookresources

Journaling

I have to admit I hated journaling at the beginning of my spiritual journey. I had some traumatic events around the result of writing my true feelings and actions. Maybe you have your own hang-ups around writing. It's funny that now I'm writing my first book! Though I'll admit, as I'm writing it at this moment, I'm definitely using voice typing! Yet, when it's time to face shadows or take proper care of myself, putting pen (or a fancy felt tip marker) to paper is what takes me there. Here are some powerful and quick journaling ideas to get you started or keep you going!

How To

Gratitude

There's a reason this trend is so trending and trendy. It's because it freaking works. In the moment you're reflecting on your gratitude, you're not able to feel any other emotion. Gratitude is powerful. The more minutes a day you start feeling grateful about the tiniest shit in your life, the happier you will be. I started my gratitude Journal by writing 10 things I was grateful for every single morning. It took about 90 seconds and was my daily non-negotiable practice for almost a year. This is the easiest self-care or spiritual habit to start, so don't sleep on it!

Rage on the Page

This feels hella good! One of my fave spiritual teachers, Gabby Bernstein, taught me this one. This works when you're angry or frustrated about something. Set a timer for 10 minutes and write as fast as you can all the thoughts popping into your head. Always bring it back to what's triggering your feelings of anger, frustration, or irritation. I promise you that on the other side of that 10 minutes, you'll feel better and have more clarity on what is actually bothering you. Then, you can face it head-on and either accept or change it.

Automatic Writing

If you're struggling to find answers, automatic writing will take you exactly where you need to go. Automatic writing is the practice of writing the messages of your higher self or Spirit guides. You can automatic write with whoever you set the intention to connect with.

- Set a timer for 5 to 7 minutes

- Take a deep breath and ask whoever you're connecting with to speak slowly enough for you to be able to write it down.

- Ask your question, or say, "What do I need to know right now related to _____?"

- Take another deep breath and start writing everything that pops into your head.

- Do your absolute best to get out of your own way, not overthink what's coming through, and just write.

The answers, insight, and wisdom that come through will sometimes astound you. Sometimes, it confirms what you already knew to be true.

Faith

Faith is the deepest spiritual self-care practice there is. I'm not talking about blind faith; I'm talking about faith with discernment. Faith while looking at any and all shreds of evidence that you live in a supportive Universe. Your faith is your belief that there is, in fact, an intelligent, benevolent force that you're a part of. One that's much bigger than you. If you're reading this book, I know you already believe that.

Religion can kind of make it twisted for you. Religion often focuses on external things. Ensuring that you follow the rules of someone you're supposed to worship. Faith is not about worship. Faith is about trusting that your spirituality will come from within you as long as you pay attention to it. Practicing your faith can look like going for a walk in nature or like fervent prayer. Faith can look like taking a deep breath and knowing that even though things seem chaotic right now, they'll work out in your favor. For your highest good and for the highest good of all.

Diet

One of the best things about being a human and a physical body is food. Food is delicious, and we cannot forget the primary function of food, which is to fuel your body. Some people are "Eat to Live" oriented. They eat the healthiest foods that will optimize their body performance. Some people are "Live to Eat" oriented, where they idolize junk food and rich foods. Most people fall somewhere between the two.

I'm not here to tell you exactly what to eat or what diet is right for you. By diet, I mean the types of food you eat, not fad diets or going on a diet. The best information I can give you is to do your own research and back it up with how you feel in your body. Refined sugar is inflammatory. Several "foods" are genetically modified or sterilized to the point of no longer being nutritious.

Read labels like it's your job. Go for the products that have the simplest and fewest ingredients possible. Fast food restaurants are evil (just kidding). They literally design their food in a lab to be addictive, so it's not a good idea. According to Healthline.com, frequent consumption of junk food may lead to dopamine tolerance. This means that a person will have to eat even more junk food to avoid going into withdrawal.

Beyond that, follow your instincts and trust your intuition. I know that you know that there may be some foods or substances that are no longer serving you. Take baby steps or go cold turkey to cut them from your life. Transforming your relationship with food is no small task. It's full of feelings and shadows. Especially if you engage in emotional eating or have struggled with eating disorders. This is where the Shadow Work part of the book will help you. If food is one of your demons, apply your food struggles or body image issues to the guided "how to heal your shadows" exercise.

All that said, I'll share a bit about my journey with food and hope it gives you some perspective. I don't have all the answers when it comes to nutrition, but I've done a lot of work on myself on this subject.

What My Journey from Veganism to Intuitive Eating Taught Me.

Before my initial spiritual awakening, I was on the standard American diet. I ate a lot of processed foods and fast foods and drank a lot of alcohol. Like, a lot of alcohol. I was a bartender. I drank a cup of coffee every morning to wake up and a glass of wine every night to wind down. This destructive cycle ended a few years before that first psychic fair. By the time I started doing spiritual work, I'd already given up caffeine. I found that it spiked my feelings of anxiety, and the more I backed off on it, the more sensitive I became to it.

Early on in my spiritual journey, I decided to become vegan. Meat carries a heavier vibration than fruits, vegetables, and other plant-based foods. Also, some research illustrates the emotional and health benefits of giving up animal products.

I was low-key high and mighty about the whole thing, which happens in a lot of vegan communities. It's understandable that you would feel like you are walking the moral high ground as a vegan. But being judgy is not walking any type of high ground. When people would say that they needed meat to be healthy, I would scoff and roll my eyes. That was until I became pregnant with my first child.

I was a full vegan for 2 years, and honestly, it felt great in my body. I had plenty of energy. I could smell meat cooking and pass on it with no problem despite the fact that I'd grown up eating it. Giving up cheese took me a while, but eventually, my palate accepted dairy substitutes. But then I got pregnant. The first time I went to a bougie burger restaurant as a pregnant woman, the smell of the meat almost made me swoon. I was salivating, and I could tell my body was sending me a message of what it wanted.

I felt conflicted. Yet I knew the truth of my body intelligence. I decided to follow my intuition, trust my body, and eat the damn burger. I swear I almost had an eating orgasm. I know there are influencers out there who say you can be vegan and have a very healthy pregnancy, birth, and baby. I don't want to disagree with their experience. But I can also embrace the logic that to create flesh and blood, consuming it can be helpful and healthful.

I'm still in my childbearing/breastfeeding years as I write this. Eating meat still feels in alignment with my body. I still sometimes struggle with the moral and ethical question of killing. To remedy that, I've decided that I should be less disconnected from it. I plan to keep and slaughter my own chickens. This way, I don't just pick up the plastic-wrapped package of ready-prepared meat. The blood will be on my own hands, so to speak. I'll face the emotional and mental repercussions of harvesting my own meat from time to time.

I'm not saying you have to go to this extreme to not be a hypocrite as a meat eater. But it's definitely important to know where your food comes from. To have that physical connection to the life of the animal who is nourishing you. To honor them and thank them for their sacrifice to support you and your purposes in the world. It feels intuitive and almost ancestral for me to live this way.

But, if one day I feel called to be a vegetarian again, or even vegan, I will listen to my body. I encourage and invite you to do the same. If you feel good being vegan, and your body, energy levels, hormones, etc., are functioning optimally, be vegan. But don't be judgy of the people who aren't. It's true that factory farming has totally fucked up our environment and our relationship with the meat we eat. But we don't need to throw out the baby with the bathwater.

If you want to eat meat, or if your body is urging you to, vote with your dollar and eat as local and organic as possible. Increase your standards and quality of meat (and all other foods) on a regular basis. Focus on organic and local foods as much as possible in your budget. Giving your body quality food is a foundational element of spiritual self-care.

But, like, actually DO IT.

Now that you're armed with spiritual self-care practices, I want to invite you to begin incorporating them into your life.

Start with your 3-minute daily non-negotiable habit. It could be gratitude journaling, meditation, salt baths… it doesn't matter. Just pick the one that seems the most interesting or fun to you and start there.

These spiritual self-care tools will support you through any and every difficult moment. They'll help you celebrate all your highlights as well.

I started this part of the book with spiritual self-care practices. Yet the spiritual self-care mindset is even more important than the practices themselves. Cultivate a spiritual self-care mindset, and the practices become easier and more effective. Let's dive into the most important mindset shift you will ever make. Bold statement, and I stand by it.

Chapter 15:
Spiritual Self-care Mindset

I never felt safe in my body, but for years, I didn't realize that was the actual issue. Instead, I'd use various substances to numb my feelings of anxiety, or I'd ignore my body in various ways. There were so many things about my body that I found lacking, annoying, and even disgusting. The biggest way I'd numb out was self-denial.

Something shocking would happen, or I'd be in a super stressful situation. But on the outside, I'd appear completely calm. For many years, I even fooled myself into thinking I was calm and nothing was ever a big deal.

I remember getting into a car accident with my mom as a teenager. I looked at my terrified younger siblings calmly, saying, "It's okay. Everything's okay." I bravely climbed out of the car and helped them do the same. Only when my dad arrived on the scene did I finally start shaking and experiencing the extent of my fear.

Many people have commended me on my ability to appear calm in chaotic or stressful situations, so I kept it up. There's a difference between:

- Being calm and peaceful in a chaotic situation

And

- Being in a perpetual "freeze state"

I mean freeze in the context of the fight, flight, or freeze nervous system response.

It all began in childhood, during any one of my mom's fits of rage. She'd start on her rampage, and I'd freeze. My soul would leave my body a little bit so that my heart wouldn't break. There was also some physical abuse in my household, as I know there was for many of you. Nothing crazy. But definitely spanking, some slapping across the face, hair pulling, things like that.

By my teens, I got used to overriding my body's signals. Sexual experiences furthered my feeling of being unsafe in my body. I had several more car accidents throughout my teen and young adult years. This only exacerbated my fear of the world around me. And fear of the "mean people" who were looking to take something out on me.

When I first came across information on empaths and spiritual protection, I sighed with relief. Putting that bubble of golden light around myself felt empowering for a while. Until the experiences I was trying to protect myself from continued to happen. Confused, I thought I needed to use a more intense form of spiritual protection, like herbs, crystals, or spells.

So I did all those things. The scary experiences, unstable people, and chaos continued to manifest. Eventually, I got curious and started looking for answers. I stumbled across a few spiritual truths I'd learned. I started to apply them to this concept of safety and spiritual protection. What I found blew my mind. It started my journey toward embracing what I call the spiritual self-care mindset.

What's the Spiritual Self Care Mindset?

The spiritual self-care mindset, at its core, is about cultivating an inner sense of safety. First, I'll explain the difference between safety and protection. It's subtle but impactful.

You'll hear many spiritual teachers and practitioners preach the value of spiritual protection. Especially those who speak to empaths. Bubbles of light, shields/shielding, protection crystals, and even protection spells. They believe in it wholeheartedly.

I do believe that spiritual protection can be useful when you're first starting out. When you're first cultivating a true sense of inner safety. But spiritual protection can only get you so far. Let's start with the difference between "safety" and "protect."

Safety vs. Protect

Safety is a noun, most often understood as a state of being, while to protect something is a verb, a state of action. You would only need to protect something or practice protection if something was unsafe or if you felt unsafe.

Let me state once more: safety is a state of being. So, the state of being safe is either something you are, or you are not. When you protect yourself, this means that at some level of belief, you do not feel safe. Whether that means you don't feel safe in a situation or certain environment, or you don't feel safe in your body.

Now, you understand the baseline difference in the concepts of safety versus protection. Here are two spiritual lessons to help you understand how practicing protection doesn't actually keep you safe. In fact, it does just the opposite.

The Law of Attraction

The law of attraction is a spiritual concept that states:

- We live in an energetic universe

- Our thoughts and feelings are also energetic

- What we think, feel, and believe attract the things, people, and events we experience in our reality.

This is a very simplistic definition of the law of attraction. Ultimately, your beliefs are what attract and co-create your reality. This is why so many people try to manifest, and it doesn't work. You can't just think your way into something you want. You have to truly believe that you're worthy of it, that it's good for you, and that it can come to you.

We talked a lot about your beliefs in the shadow work part of the book. Let's bridge your understanding of limiting beliefs with your sense of safety. What are you attracting into your life based on any limiting beliefs you may have? Any lack of safety you may feel in your body or surroundings will show up in your life.

What I'm saying is that if a part of you doesn't believe you're safe, you'll attract things to confirm that belief. If you're practicing spiritual protection, you're taking action to keep yourself safe. On some level, that means you don't believe you're safe. And so, because the law of attraction is neutral, you'll continue to attract experiences and people that confirm your lack of safety.

I know this is a big pill to swallow. It's a realization that I continue to integrate on deeper and deeper levels to this day. I invite you to begin the transformation of your lack of safety by affirming the truth of your safety. It might be hard to do that when you look around you and see criminals, corrupt elites, and people in your life who cause you drama. I'll help you get there with another spiritual truth.

Unity Consciousness

"We are one." This is something that people in spiritual circles say very often. It can sound very cute, loving, and light-like, but it's not just something we say as we Kumbaya around the campfire. Unity consciousness is the ultimate spiritual truth. At one level of dimensionality, every single being is an aspect of God, the Universe, or Source energy. This Source energy contains everything within it and everyone.

In the human experience, we get caught up in separation. Separation between individual people and animals. Separation between incarnations, souls, soul families, and oversouls. While all these points of separation are true, the paradox is that we are also ONE consciousness.

When you begin to understand Oneness on a metaphysical and physical level, you can accept that:

- Every person in your life, every single person you encounter daily, is an aspect of you.

Yes, you still keep your individuality, your sovereign soul, and your physical being. And also you are one with everyone. That doesn't mean that you're ONE only with the people who agree with you. Or that you're ONE only with the people who treat you kindly.

You are also ONE with those you disagree with. With the people you consider to be evil. With extraterrestrial beings and galactic consciousness. Unity consciousness is not subjective. When you begin to accept this, you can understand that when you fear being attacked, harmed, or traumatized by:

- Family or friends
- Strangers
- Politicians
- Criminals
- Mobs
- Or even demons

That your fear is only of yourself. That your ability to be traumatized is directly related to your belief system.

This truth is empowering. You have control over:

- Your consciousness
- Your belief systems
- What you manifest in your reality

There are things you may have agreed to take part in before you came into this life that are/were traumatic. But even these things can change if you believe it. And if it's in alignment with the highest good for all.

People in your life who cause you pain are simply a reflection of the pain within you. The ways in which you're at war with yourself. Once you begin to integrate the truth of unity consciousness married with the law of attraction, you can set yourself free. No matter what your family, partner, friends, or governments do, it'll never get in the way of you being all you're meant to be in this life. Period.

We'll talk a little bit more about using boundaries rather than protection in a moment. For now, I want to bring it home with the one affirmation you MUST take with you beyond this book. The one affirmation to rule them all!

The Safest Place to be is Where You Are

I want to arm you with the affirmation you need to say to yourself every day. It will begin to transform your belief into one of self-safety. Here it is:

THE SAFEST PLACE TO BE IS WHERE I AM.

Repeat this affirmation in your mind three times and then out loud three times. Notice what comes up for you. Notice the response you have in your body. Are you rolling your eyes? Are you uncomfortable? Does it feel empty? Don't worry. The more you do your Shadow Work, the louder your intuition will shout this affirmation from the depths of your soul.

You can't just say, "I'm safe." You have to BELIEVE it.

Saying, "the safest place to be is where you are," will not stop you from having challenging experiences. Ones that test this new belief you're implanting. Your mind and unresolved trauma will continue to manifest experiences confirming your lack of safety. You may have developed several beliefs that confirm this lack of safety. You may have manifested many traumas in your life that have double-confirmed this lack of safety. So, it will take a while for you to believe that you're safe within your body.

As you begin to believe in your safety, things will continue to test you. You will continue to experience traumatic events, either small or big. But your experience of them will transform. You'll no longer feel traumatized when crazy things are happening around you. You'll become the eye of the storm. You'll be able to tell the difference between inner peace and the "freeze state." You'll be a force of peace and power as the human collective continues to suffer with feelings of victimhood and lack of safety.

It's not inhumane or inconsiderate of you to feel peace. It's not selfish of you to transform your sense of safety while others continue to be victimized and feel unsafe. In fact, it's crucial that you continue to cultivate and spread this belief of safety. So that you can illustrate what is possible to everyone else in your life and, if you feel called, the world.

We cannot feel sorry for people and expect this will heal them. Compassion is different from codependency. Be compassionate while still holding healthy boundaries and cultivating your sense of safety. This is much more effective than sitting in victim solidarity with your fellow man, woman, or even child. Hold the line of true safety, sovereignty, and self-empowerment. Hold space while honoring your boundaries.

You may be wondering, "Okay, Ciara. I get it. I need to cultivate this sense of safety. That it's possible because of the spiritual truths you outlined. But what the hell do I actually do in my day-to-day life?" I got you.

Chapter 16:
Boundaries Over Protection

The words and concepts you use every day shape and influence your life more than you know. Being precise with the types of words you use when you speak about yourself and others is crucial.

Without becoming a cliche talking about "the good old days," I do want to state that today, we're experiencing a breakdown of words and language. Everything is shorthand, abbreviated. We use slang words to describe things that they don't actually mean.

Words are spells. Every time you speak, write, or type, know that you're casting energy. Energy that will manifest in your physical world. I want to make that clear as we move into this concept of boundaries over protection. They're not the same thing.

Setting healthy boundaries holds different energy than protecting yourself. When setting a boundary, you're letting yourself, others, and the universe know what you will and won't accept in your space. When practicing spiritual protection, you're putting up a bubble or hoping/praying that your boundaries don't get violated.

Boundaries hold the energy of sovereignty and self-empowerment. Spiritual protection holds the energy of fear and victim mentality. Spiritual protection is the people pleaser's boundary. As an empath, I know you sometimes struggle to say no (or all the time). Even if you've started to practice boundaries, you struggle with setting boundaries in a healthy, direct way.

Guilt and anxiety often come up with beginner boundary setting. Becoming comfortable being "that person" who sets boundaries is a THING. Often, when an empath is practicing spiritual protection, it's because they want to set a boundary. But they're afraid to piss people off. Or they're afraid of what other people will think when they set that boundary.

Let me boldly state it this way:

- If you're about to enter into a situation where you feel like you need to practice protection, you don't actually want to be there.

- It's not in your highest good, and part of you knows that.

- You're putting a bubble around yourself or carrying some black obsidian instead of changing your situation or setting a boundary.

I challenge you to take a close look at those relationships and situations where you feel you need protection. Choose to start setting boundaries instead.

How? Let's dive into it.

Devices

You might be giving me an inner eye roll, but I promise you this is the best place to start. Once you can set boundaries with yourself, it will be much easier to set boundaries with other people.

I know you know that we all spend way too much time in front of screens. I don't want to demonize screens. They enable us to do amazing work. We can connect with each other at lightning speed and find vast amounts of knowledge at our fingertips. Your devices are valuable tools. But you need to ensure that you're using those tools and that those tools are not ruling you.

Take an honest look at your life, lifestyle, and job or career. Where are the places where you can set boundaries with your devices? By devices, I mean smartphones, ipads, computers, and televisions.

Some examples:

- Keep your phone in sleep mode for at least an hour in the morning. Connect with yourself before diving into everybody else's energy. Your emails, social media, etc.

- Decide on a certain time in the evening when you plug your phone into the charger and let it go for the rest of the night.

- Set time limits for certain apps. The same idea can apply to your tablet and your computer.

The TV is a little bit more amorphous. But I will tell you right now that watching TV shows and movies all the time will get in your way if you have big goals. If something pops up that you feel drawn to, or if there are documentaries that will expand your knowledge, indulge. But there's so much content that it could get you spending your entire life distracted, plugged in, and living a status quo life. Right in that same vein is setting boundaries with the type of content you consume.

Content

Everything you see with your eyes and hear with your ears is programming. It literally programs your brain and your being. When you watch something, your body doesn't know the difference between that trauma happening to the person on screen and the trauma happening to you. According to SkywayBehavioralHealth.com, experts agree that violence seen in different mediums, including television, can impact mental health.

This is why, after 9 years on my spiritual journey, I no longer watch reality TV or scary movies. I even find it difficult to watch super suspenseful movies. It's kind of a joy kill because I do love a good cerebral thriller. The more sensitive my intuition gets, the more sensitive I become to certain content. Sometimes, I have to take a break from political commentary. Even if you feel you're on the right side of history, there's a lot of anger and fear on every side of the issue.

All this to say, take a close look at the types of content you consume on a regular basis. Are you often watching women bash their husbands or their lives? Are you watching reality television that is rife with manufactured drama and superficiality? Are you often watching horror films (people who are not safe)? Do you watch porn? All these are programming that keep you from living an empowered, enlightened, and embodied life.

The type of programming you watch will be what you see mirrored in your reality. It'll be what you experience and expect because it's what you're programming yourself to see around you. I'm not saying you need to become a total Pollyanna and only watch things with rainbows and unicorns. I'm saying to take a close and conscious look with a critical eye at the things you're watching and consuming.

You may feel like you need to watch the news (or alternative news) to stay up to date on what's happening in the world. Remember that what you see happening in the world is a reflection of the beliefs, fears, shadows, and the light within you. Go on a month-long media detox while also diving deep into Shadow Work. I assure you the types of things you manifest will change when you come out of that detox.

Spend a few months setting boundaries with your technology. Edit the content you consume/program yourself with. Then, you'll be ready (even if you don't feel ready) to set boundaries with the people in your life.

People & Relationships

Boundaries in your relationships are definitely some next-level spiritual self-care. It can be challenging if you were never taught to set boundaries growing up. Or if you didn't even have an understanding of the concept of boundaries. There are entire books written on setting boundaries with people. I won't attempt to be completely comprehensive here. But I will give you some tips that have helped me set boundaries and embrace myself as someone who does that.

Boundaries don't have to be all or nothing. You may feel resistance to setting boundaries with people because:

- You feel like you either need to allow them to be close to you

- Or have no contact and no relationship whatsoever.

There are so many shades of gray between those two extremes. Explore and discover the level of contact with someone who makes you feel energized, empowered, and at peace.

You may need to set boundaries around how often you see someone. Or how often you're comfortable with them coming to see you. You may need to set boundaries around the frequency of communication with them. Or around the types of communication you'll engage in with them.

For example, you might enjoy talking to your mom once or a few times a week but don't want to hear about her drama. Drama is different from true difficulty or vulnerability. You might be willing to help your partner talk through something that they're going through. However, at a certain point, you don't want to be their therapist. You also need them to reciprocate and hold space for you.

Setting boundaries with people can be a tricky process. I don't want you to expect yourself to be perfect or even good at it right away. When you're first setting boundaries, those boundaries can be a little abrasive or rigid. Sometimes, you realize you haven't set a strong enough boundary and must set it again.

Then, there will be those special people in your life who are natural boundary crossers. People who have no understanding of boundaries themselves. They make it impossible to get around having to set boundaries with them.

I have one such person in my life; I call them my spiritual boundary teacher. This person constantly tests my boundaries. Even when I set a clear boundary, they'll respect it for anywhere between 1 to 3 weeks. Then, they begin trying to test the boundary again. It's maddening at times. Yet the amount of help and support that this person offers to my life is valuable.

This person also does not presume to tell me how to live my life. They don't make their support contingent on my willingness to live my life as they see fit. For these reasons, I have done so much inner work to allow them to continue to be close to me and support me in my life. I'm still learning how to be uncomfortable and set some freaking boundaries.

It's up to you to decide which relationships are reciprocal, healthy enough, or valuable enough for you to continue to draw boundaries. Or if you need to cut your losses and move on without them in your life.

When you're setting boundaries, you don't have to have a cut-and-dry conversation with the person you're setting boundaries with. Often, setting boundaries energetically is a great way to begin.

For example:

You've been:

- Following someone closely on social media
- Interacting with them through text message
- And seeing them in person.

You can begin by muting them on social media. Then, take your time to answer their text messages. Stop initiating hanging out with them in person. You're not going out of your way to let them know you're setting a boundary with them. And yet they will still feel the absence of your energy in their life.

This may cause them to reach out more at first. Or they may ask you why you haven't been as interested in the relationship. At that point, you can choose whether you're honest with them or simply tell them you've had a lot going on lately.

You need to use your intuition to decide which people belong in your inner circle. If they do, it's worth being honest with them. If they don't, you don't owe them anything (they also don't owe you anything). You can keep it very surface level if that helps you set the boundary. I always recommend as much honesty as you can manage, even if it's uncomfortable. But I would rather you set the boundary and feel empowered and at peace than continue to feel victimized or create drama. Allow yourself a period of grieving the relationship that could have been.

I totally get that putting a bubble around yourself would be much easier. Remember that spiritual protection is the people-pleaser version of boundaries. You can't continue to take the easy way out and still love yourself. Someone who loves themselves does the hard thing that creates true freedom and inner peace. You're developing and trusting your intuition. Using your intuition to create the life you desire. The life you're meant to live. The life that's possible for you. Nothing less than true freedom and true self-love will do. Set those boundaries, girl!

For some easy-to-follow boundary-setting scripts that you can use in any relationship, visit www.ciararubin.com/ yakbookresources

Work & Jobs

Setting boundaries at work and setting boundaries in your relationships are similar. Of course, jobs have certain requirements and things that you can't get around. I often say that every job or even entrepreneurial career has a "shit sandwich." An aspect of it that kind of sucks; a chore that you have to put up with to have the positives.

You have to decide whether you can eat the "shit sandwich" (or sandwiches) that comes along with your career. Aside from that, you can set boundaries with your bosses and coworkers in many ways.

Obvi, you still need to complete the tasks laid out in your job description. You can go a little bit above and beyond if you're looking to grow within that company. But you don't need to be a martyr, and you don't need to get resentful for doing other people's jobs besides yours.

A lot of this comes down to being honest with yourself and deciding if it's time to leave your job. Or you can finally start your business while still supporting yourself with your job.

Boundaries with Spiritual Beings

In step one of this book, you learned about clairvoyance, opening your third eye, and the fear often associated with all the above. I mentioned that you can set boundaries with the spirit world, so let's expand on that here.

You are the master of your own domain and your physical reality. You are co-creating your physical reality with:

- Spirit
- Your higher self
- God
- Your angels and guides
- Source energy

You get the idea! You have the ability to set boundaries with energetic beings and people.

Yes, ghosts are real; interdimensional beings are real. I've experienced and met them myself as a result of opening my third eye. It's true; there are dark, negative energies available and willing to interact with you. But you're not a victim of this.

Number one, where your focus goes, GROWS. If you choose to focus on encountering negative beings, you'll experience more of that.

Number two, you have the ability to decide what you will and won't allow in your space.

Some people practice mediumship. They allow ghosts to pass over people in their space. I have mediumship abilities, just as you and anyone else do. And yet, I choose not to interact with those types of energies and beings on a regular basis.

I often set boundaries with ghosts. I let them know that I'm not available for interaction. Or at least asking them to have the courtesy to come back during the daylight. What is up with entities and spiritual beings always trying to get at me in the dark?! Those are not my freaking office hours!

All jokes aside, you can set boundaries with ghosts, shadow beings, and any other type of negative being you can imagine.

You can even set boundaries with interdimensional beings. Due to the laws of free will that govern this Universe, all beings must respect your free will. If you're not inviting them to inhabit your space, they have to leave.

Here's the how-to:

1. You get the sense that there's a ghost, a passed-over loved one, a shadow being, or another being you don't want in your space.

2. All you have to do is either in your head or out loud, tell them to *go away*. Let them know that you are sovereign and the master of your space.

3. Imagine a white portal opening wherever you are. See them exiting through the portal.

4. Burn some sage or palo santo, clearing the space afterward for good measure.

You're not the victim of anybody, including spiritual beings. With all this boundary talk, you might feel a bit daunted by it all. I know I was when I first started setting boundaries, and sometimes I still am. You can take it one step at a time.

No More People Pleasing

In Step 1, I talked about the #empathproblem of people pleasing.

Most empaths who struggle with people pleasing grew up in a home where they had to manage the emotions of their caregivers to stay safe. They learned to ignore their own true feelings. If they expressed intense anger, sadness, or even joy, their caregiver may have either:

- Emotionally abandoned them (shame them, ignore them, cold shoulder, etc.)

- Physically abandoned them by walking out of the room or using physical abuse.

A child should not have to be responsible for the emotions of an adult. This dynamic produces codependency. It also makes it hard to have healthy relationships as they grow into adults themselves. Does this dynamic sound familiar to you? Perhaps you're realizing at this moment that you experienced this dynamic. Either way, it means that you have an abandonment wound.

Abandonment wounds are extremely, and unfortunately, common. This is because many of our parents and grandparents didn't get the emotional support they needed as children. They continued that cycle onto us. You get to be a cycle breaker in this life. To become aware of this abandonment wound shadow. Because of your bravery, your children won't have to experience the same struggles in their adult lives and relationships as you did/do.

Struggles like getting into relationships with people who are energetic vampires. People who drain you and make you responsible for their emotions. The friends or family members who are always calling or texting you about their problems.

Another struggle that comes from the abandonment wound is codependency. When you're codependent, your happiness is dependent on the emotional state of others. Codependent dynamics in romantic relationships, friendships, and family relationships are unhealthy. It can prevent you (and them) from becoming all of who you are.

There's a difference between having compassion for someone and being codependent. Listening to someone in their vulnerable moments and sharing your vulnerable moments with them can be healthy. But when you're codependent, you must spend lots of time together all the time. Because when you don't, you may start to see dysfunctional parts of the relationship. Once you see the truth, you must start setting healthy boundaries. Boundaries and codependency do not mix.

I do not intend to pass any judgment on you if these themes come up in your life. In fact, I'm sharing them and have such insight about them because they're themes that often come up in my life. I'm a recovering people pleaser and recovering codependent. I used to struggle with one-sided friendships. I stayed in unhealthy romantic relationships for way too long. Serial monogamy, anyone?

Once I became aware, I began to use Shadow Work on my abandonment wounds. One by one, I took a look at each person and situation that had created and reopened these abandonment wounds. I either alchemized them with catharsis, set healthy boundaries, practiced forgiveness, or all the above.

This is what I recommend you do. Take an honest look at all your relationships. All the promises you make that you either can't fulfill or feel resentful while you do. Have the courage to pattern interrupt. Break the cycle of people pleasing, and rise to your full potential.

Practice It

Keep practicing the affirmation:

The safest place to be is where you are.

Start small by setting boundaries with your devices and the content you consume.

Start setting indirect or direct boundaries with the people in your life that reflect what you will and won't accept.

I promise you that even if it feels messy, and even if you don't do it perfectly, setting boundaries in your life will:

- Make you love and respect yourself more
- Give you more energy to do the things that you actually want to do in your day-to-day life
- Give you true sovereignty and self-empowerment.

For easy-to-follow boundary-setting scripts you can use in any relationship, visit ***www.ciararubin.com/yakbookresources***

Ultimately, the spiritual self-care mindset and your spiritual self-care practices will make you trust yourself and, by extension, trust your intuition.

Get it. Do it. Be it.

My hope for you is that you take it slow and make spiritual self-care a part of your lifestyle. That you take these practices and test them out one at a time to see which ones bring you the most joy and peace.

I hope that even when you don't feel like taking care of yourself on a spiritual level, you do it anyway. That your action motivates more spiritual self-care and helps you trust that you've got yourself. That no matter what you go through, no matter what shadow you're facing, you have the tools to take care of yourself and get yourself through it. Of course, spirit is right by your side, supporting you the whole way. You're never alone.

You are powerful. It is safe for you to be powerful. It's time to move into the final step of developing and trusting your intuition: validation.

Intuition and spirituality are the newest frontiers for this current iteration of humanity. You'll need validation in the physical world that your intuition is real and accurate so you can trust it. In the final step of this book, we're gonna get you that real-world validation, and it's gonna be hella fun!

STEP 4:
Intuition Validation

Chapter 17:
My Secret Credit Card

So now we'll talk about the $7,000 secret credit card. In step 3, I shared with you how my marriage almost ended due to my spiritual awakening and decision to follow my calling. I shared the ultimatum I gave my husband to either come with me to California or stay behind.

There's one more aspect of that part of my life to share with you as we begin to talk about intuition validation. The story I'm about to share with you may seem extreme. But my intuition kept guiding me forward. My trust in my intuition was validated and rewarded.

I was exploring many aspects of my spirituality:

- Past and parallel lives
- The Lost civilizations of Atlantis and Lemuria
- Galactic consciousness.

I decided to have a session with a powerful and well-known spiritual teacher, who I won't name. I was very proud to secure a session with this person, as their resume and personality put stars in my eyes.

I sat across from him, and immediately, without any prompting, he asked me how I felt about California. Que me: being stunned! I'd recently given my husband the California ultimatum. We talked about many things in the session, including my lifetimes in Atlantis. Near the end of the conversation, he asked me how I felt about Egypt.

Egypt has been very special to me since I was a small child. I have no idea when or why the actual interest sparked. I do remember always having a fascination with ancient Egypt. I collected books and card decks all about Egypt. When I was in high school, we had to write a research paper and develop a demonstration to go with it. I chose mummification.

My dad took me to the grocery store, and we bought all the animal organs they had for sale. The ones that most people don't even look at, let alone buy. We got several of them, some red Jello and some bandages. I "mummified" a classmate for my demonstration. I'm sure my peers were totally grossed out, but maybe intrigued?

So when this spiritual teacher asked me about Egypt, it was a deep childhood recognition. He shared that he took groups of people on tours to Egypt and asked me if I'd go with him on his next spiritual retreat. I knew in my bones that I had to go with him, but there was only one problem.

I didn't have anywhere near the money to go on this trip. With the rocky state of my marriage, I knew there was no way my husband would agree to contribute to me going off and finding myself in Egypt. But I had to go. So, I told the spiritual teacher that I would find a way. We got off the call, and I immediately (secretly) applied for a credit card. I didn't have great credit then, so I had no idea if I'd get approved or what amount I'd get approved for.

I waited a couple of days and received the news that I'd been approved for a $7,000 limit! Floored, I took it as another sign that I was doing something I was meant to do. Without telling my husband, I paid for the trip in full, booked my flights, and started planning.

The day I finally came clean was almost as horrific as giving him the California ultimatum. I felt shame, despair, and yet still an indignant righteousness. I was claiming independence and doing what I wanted to do. Refusing to let him and his practicality hold me back. I made a terrible decision when it came to the immediate health and strength of my marriage. But following my gut and booking that trip to Egypt was later validated.

We sold almost all our possessions as we prepared to embark on our RV adventure to California. We sold the house we both worked hard to renovate. The money we made on our house more than paid off the entire credit card bill from the trip to Egypt and my time there.

I definitely wouldn't recommend getting a secret credit card. Yet, though it was completely impractical, Spirit still had my back. The California ultimatum is what made the Egypt trip possible. Furthermore, the RV adventure itself 100% saved my marriage.

During our 14 months of travel, my husband and I worked together to navigate the country. We saw beautiful sights and explored six national parks. He came along with me to several spiritual sites and events. I did my best to stay grounded, develop better money habits, and devote myself to him, two feet in.

My plan all along was to move to California to escape from the southeast United States. Much of the American spiritual awakening revolution is happening around Los Angeles. I thought if I could move back to California, where I was born, all would be right. I could become who I was meant to be.

Don't get me wrong, California is an amazing place. I still consider it to be the most beautiful state in our country. Yet everything I was running from followed me there. There were more places to get smoothies and green juice. But I found that just as many people were living lives expected of them rather than their truth. Just as many people were avoiding self-awareness and Shadow Work. Even if they considered themselves to be spiritual!

This is where I learned the difference between "doing spirituality" and **being** spiritual.

All this to say, it doesn't matter where you are in the world. What matters is where you are on your own journey toward self-awareness, self-love, and integration. Right as I had this realization, my husband and I were at the tail end of our work camping position in Napa Valley. I was about 4 months pregnant with our first child. I realized that to gain a strong foundation to build a successful life, I'd need to return to the East Coast.

Before, I would have completely ignored this gut feeling. But after everything I'd been through, I knew the writing was on the wall. That it was time to go back. I'd left home with a fragmented relationship, fear, and judgment. I returned with a strong marriage, a trip to Egypt, a cross-country adventure, and a baby in my belly.

Why? Because I listened to my intuition. I encourage you to listen to your intuition, even when it seems insane and illogical. There is a time and place for logic. Yet, if you follow the voice of your intuition, I promise you will be supported.

If you take leaps of faith even though you cannot see how Spirit will support you, you will be vindicated. Your intuition will be validated. It may take time, but you always know. You always know what's best for you; you always know what path you should be following. You always know, deep down, exactly who you are and what's possible for you. It's scary and powerful, and it is safe for you to be powerful.

Let's dive into some practical ways to validate your intuition.

Chapter 18:
Why Validation?

Anytime you're learning a new skill, it's important to get validation.

- You need validation that you have what it takes to develop that skill.

- Validation that you're improving that skill over time.

- You'll need validation in the physical world that your intuition is real.

There's no shame in that. There are times and spaces for faith in your intuition. And yet, paradoxically, there are also times and spaces for physical, real-world validation.

The intuitive senses are "extra senses." Meaning that they're often more subtle of an experience. So having tangible proof that what you're feeling, seeing, hearing, or knowing is real... is everything, especially at the beginning of your journey.

Intuition validation is your ticket to trust. To trust your intuition, you'll need proof on the reg from the outside world that you're on the right track.

Intuitive nudges, signs, and downloads will come at you from everywhere. It's time to understand exactly what your intuition is telling you. To get the proof in your physical reality that you are, in fact, receiving those messages. I'll dive into several practical ways to do this, but first, you need to understand a few crucial things.

Quality of your message = Quality of your vibe

I stated this earlier in the book, but I wanna drive it home.

The quality and clarity of the messages you'll receive from your intuition and the quality and clarity of the validation you'll receive are directly correlated to your vibrational frequency.

In other words, the more Shadow Work you do and the better you take care of yourself, the louder and clearer your intuition will be.

You can try to use all the other tools I've given you in this book to develop your intuition. But if you don't work on your frequency or get down and dirty with your Shadow Work, you'll never fully trust it. You may be able to fake it until you make it, but sooner or later, you'll create chaos and destruction in your life. This is because you won't follow your intuition from an authentic place.

If you want:

- Real-world validation
- Physical proof
- Money
- Aligned relationships
- Fantastic opportunities

You have to cultivate a higher vibration. That doesn't mean shifting into toxic positivity. Clutching your crystals and blessing everyone with love and light. If you're going to create the life meant for you and achieve everything possible, you need to do the work to back it up.

This is especially important if you consider yourself a lightworker. Or if you help others as a career or would like to. If you're going to help other people move through challenges in their lives, you sure as hell better be walking your talk. Use your intuition to look at yourself in the mirror and deal with your challenges. Ok, I think you get it!

One of the simplest ways to validate your intuition almost seems silly, but it isn't.

Entertaining the idea of a spiritual experience

When you were a kid, did anyone ever tell you, "Your eyes were just playing tricks on you?" Did they tell you you were "just imagining something?" These are some very simple but powerful ways we, as a society, shut down our intuition.

Maybe you saw a shadow out of the corner of your eye or a sparkle of light. I won't discount that it could be a trick of the light. And I also invite you to explore the very true possibility that it wasn't a trick of the light.

When developing your intuition, you need to show that you're willing to suspend your disbelief. You need to allow the way you perceive the world around you to shift. Remembering that everything around you is energy that's moving and breathing. Even the seemingly inanimate objects are made of atoms in constant motion.

Entertaining the idea of a spiritual experience will allow them into your awareness. I assure you that you're already having "spiritual experiences" all the time. Spiritual experiences don't just start happening once you're aware of them. They happen constantly.

You're a spiritual being having a human experience. Everything is a spiritual experience. Of course, I'm talking about the experiences that happen within the more subtle intuitive senses, but you get the idea.

This small but important shift of opening your awareness and allowing the possibility of experiencing something "beyond this physical world" is the best first step toward intuition validation.

Question with an open mind

I'm not saying to throw caution and logic to the wind and believe every little thing you feel and see. It's important to balance your intuition with your logic. To be somewhat skeptical as you allow your intuition to unfold and show you the proof of what you're sensing. Question yourself and your intuition with an open mind. Allow your definition of what it means to be human to expand.

Temper your expansion with integration. Integration is paramount. You must integrate your spiritual experiences and realizations into your personality and beliefs. If you only focus on expanding your intuition, you won't get anywhere. Shadow Work is a powerful and important form of integration.

Spiritual expansion and intuitive downloads can be fun, even addictive. But if you don't take the time to integrate them, you're another righteous Guru who isn't walking their talk.

Spiritual Experiences in Egypt

Learning to trust and validate my intuition paved the way for all my mystical experiences while on a spiritual retreat to Egypt in 2016. It's interesting because several of my family members warned me of the dangers of The Middle East. And yet, when I walked to the balcony in my Egyptian hotel room, I felt more at home than I ever have anywhere else in my life. The desert sun beamed down on my face. I breathed in the ancient frequencies of the many lifetimes I must have lived there.

We traveled in a giant bus with an armed guard most of the time, visiting Temple after Temple. Each time I entered the holy of holies, the main altar room where the high priest and priestesses would perform their rituals, I felt a sense of recognition and remembering. There were two experiences in particular that I'm going to share with you. They helped me see myself in a completely different way. First was the galactic activation in the Tomb of Ay.

We spent the early part of the day exploring the Valley of the Kings. This is a large area where many pharaohs are buried, including King Tut. Everyone in the group felt like we were anticipating something. As we toured the last tomb, my legs and knees weirdly started to shake and vibrate. The energies were palpable and powerful.

Next, we ventured into the valley of the baboons. A lesser-known area where many high priests and priestesses are buried. Our retreat leader led us to a locked door with bars on it. The guard put his arms on our leader's shoulders and said a prayer. Then, he unlocked the door and allowed us to descend into the burial chamber.

This was the Tomb of the High Priest Ay. A man of great power and spiritual prowess. He was a high priest serving the mysterious Pharaoh Akhenaten and then his son Tutankhamun after him.

When we reached the giant sarcophagus at the bottom of the tunnel, we made a circle around it and held hands. Our leader informed us that we would turn out all the lights and perform a chanting and meditation ritual. With three claps of his hands, we bathed in complete darkness. We began to chant "OM" at the same pitch.

After what felt like three or four minutes, I heard a voice in my head telling me to take my pitch higher, so I did. The instruction repeated itself again and again. I didn't want to stand out too much. The sounds I was making were very different from everyone else's. And yet, the voice in my head kept pushing me higher.

As I obliged, I started to feel the same shaking in my legs that I'd felt earlier. Beginning at my toes, it moved up my legs, into my torso, and then my entire body. It was almost uncontrollable. The group around me seemed to get louder and louder as I shook and convulsed while singing "OM" as high as I could. The energy pulsing through my body felt galactic and almost too much to handle.

Our leader started slowing his chanting and brought us back down to earth. As I came back into my body, I was overwhelmed with emotion and started to cry. I felt like how I felt after the Christ Light activation dream I mentioned earlier in the book. Fried. Our leader looked over at me and said, "Wow, you got a big blast there, didn't you!?" All I could do was nod.

As we came back up out of the tunnel and into the light, there was a pile of rocks right outside of our bus. One caught my attention, so I picked it up and studied it. It was in the shape of an eye, but in place of the pupil was a shape that looked like a falcon head, like the Egyptian god Horus. Horus is associated with clear-seeing and the all-seeing eye.

I put the stone in my pocket. As the rest of the day unfolded, I realized that I'd made the entire trip about gaining the approval of my retreat leader. Wanting to be seen as the most spiritually tuned in and special. I was projecting my power onto him. Not seeing all the shadows within him, he was projecting onto everyone else. I'm unsure what clarity came from that experience for the rest of the group. But from that day on, I allowed the trip to be for me and stopped trying to be the "teacher's pet."

I hope sharing this experience with you helps you understand that the people you look up to are just people. That not everyone deserves your loyalty and adoration. Discern the people walking their talk from those who are charismatically leading from their ego. You don't have to be close to the teacher to learn from them. Sometimes, you can even teach the teacher a thing or two simply by being who you are.

This new clarity about myself and my leader led to another wild experience near the end of the trip. Yet again, our group was allowed into areas where most of the general public was not.

At the beginning of the trip, our leader asked us why we thought we were here.

One of my responses was that I felt I was meant to connect with the cat beings. Many of the cat and lion goddesses the Egyptians revered were extraterrestrial beings.

It's important to note that most statues and freestanding objects have been removed from the temple complexes. They've either been stolen or taken for museums or private collections. The guard unlocked a heavy metal door and led us into a holy of holies. It shocked me to see a black granite statue of the lion-headed goddess, Sekhmet.

I felt deeply moved as we began to hold hands and chant around the statue. I could sense centuries of worship and communication with this amazing and wise being. I closed my eyes, and I was face deep in reddish-blond fur. I felt 10 years old in the vision, and as I backed up, I noticed a comb in my right hand.

It felt so real. I could smell the earthiness of the fur and sense the immense size of the creature I was caring for. I never saw the creature's face in the vision, but I heard its voice in my head say, "Hello, sister." I'm tearing up as I'm writing this and re-experiencing it.

As soon as I heard her say sister, I immediately rejected it and said, "No, I'm not worthy." She immediately retorted that I was worthy, that I was her sister, and that I must see myself as such. She then said, "You are chosen because you choose." These two simple phrases hold deep meaning and intuitive downloads that I'm honored to share with you.

First, this acknowledgment of me as her sister. It's a message that human beings are not beneath any other being. That we are meant to take our place amongst other Galactic beings. We must accept that it's safe for us to be powerful.

Yes, we are imperfect. We still kill one another, yet we have so much potential for growth, activation, and love. The only way to achieve full realization as individuals and as humanity is if we begin to accept and reach for that potential.

I believe this was Sekhmet speaking to me through another lifetime of mine. One in which I was the daughter of a priestess, tasked with caring for and worshiping this fantastic being.

Her second message, "You are chosen because you choose," is very important. Especially if you're an empath or consider yourself a lightworker. Many spiritual people get caught up in the idea of being a "Chosen One." But this message says that those chosen are simply those who choose to step into their calling. Any person can awaken to their spirituality and use their power to affect positive change in the world.

You don't have to be a certain someone from a special bloodline to:

- Consider yourself intuitive
- Develop spiritual abilities
- Be a spiritual teacher.

All you have to do is choose. Choose awakening. Choose Shadow Work. Choose to be a leader by leading yourself through the darkness and allowing your light to shine for others to do the same.

The deep love I felt from Sekhmet and the deep love I felt for her was so overwhelming. I was weeping as I chanted. As the ritual ended, I walked to her statue and bowed before it.

I know that these experiences sound fantastical. I invite you to entertain the idea with an open mind that they were real. I can't say for certain whether they were "real," but they were my experiences and felt very real to me.

The downloads I received and what I've learned from them are invaluable. Allow yourself to experience your intuition fully. You'll have your own magical and real spiritual experiences that will expand your consciousness and allow you to see yourself in a new way.

Now, you've had a few mindset and perspective shifts, and I've shared some of my own mystical experiences. Here are some practical ways to validate your intuition.

Chapter 19:
Is It Really Your Intuition, Tho?

It can be challenging to know the difference between guidance that's coming from:

- Your ego, or your smaller self

OR

- Your higher self, intuition, or your soul.

Here are some indicators:

Ideas or guidance coming from your ego will feel:

- Cautionary
- Fear-based
- Anxious
- Almost entirely logical.

Ideas or guidance coming from your higher self/intuition will feel:

- Slightly to deeply exciting
- Self-empowering

- A little (or a lot) outside of your comfort zone.

I'm sure you're a bit of an over-thinker, so don't get too caught up in this. As you practice what you've learned in this book, the voice of your intuition will speak louder and louder. It will get easier for you to understand.

Cult of Personality

To illustrate the difference between your intuition and ego, I'll tell on myself. I'll share a shadow that few people talk about until it's gone way too far. This shadow is called the cult of personality.

A long time ago, and even 20 years ago, these spiritual concepts that I'm sharing with you were taboo. They could get you ridiculed and ostracized from society. If you go back far enough, they could even get you killed. These empowering ideas and practices stayed within secret circles, societies, and mystery schools.

To spread this important knowledge, you had to be a spiritual authority. You had to have people looking up to you, almost like you were a god amongst them. This way of being and behaving would create literal cults. Groups of people blindly following a charismatic leader without questioning them. People who were gaining knowledge and some type of expansion.

But often, the power would go to the leader's head. Maybe they'd experienced some trauma that made them want to be the "most special." I talked about this special shadow in part one. The leader would treat her community like subjects in a kingdom or like worshipers. And her community was all too eager to oblige. To subjugate themselves and worship the teacher.

The expansion the teacher brought to the community was valued beyond personal boundaries. Beyond healthy behavior. You see extreme versions of this end up in the news as death and suicide cults. These are cults of personality that have gone way too far. Led by psychopaths. It can be easy to take a look at those examples and roll your eyes. Thinking that it would never happen to you, but the path to these cults starts small.

It starts with a wise and charismatic leader personality. This leader starts to share their knowledge with others. This leader has some serious spiritual skills. The ability to connect with the spiritual realms. The leader will channel information that feels expansive. Information that feels crucial for avoiding catastrophe. The leader will channel information that feels "special." And so her community will gather around her, hungry for what she'll say next.

When I was first starting out as a spiritual teacher, I shared my message online with live broadcasting. Every day, I'd go live and talk about various spiritual topics. I grew a large following. I started verbally channeling various spiritual and galactic energies.

Connecting with these energies and bringing their messages through felt amazing. The reaction of the people watching me do this felt even more amazing. So I kept doing it. People wanted more. They invited me to create a small society or circle. They'd depend on my channeling to travel and open or unlock certain energy portals.

This felt so seductive and fed my ego for breakfast, lunch, and dinner. They treated me like I was the most special. It was almost creepy how much they idolized me and put me on a pedestal. The information I was bringing through was accurate. The things I could tap into and know "without knowing" were astounding. But when I got pregnant with my first son, it became clear that what I was doing was unhealthy for them and me.

Yes, I may have access to special information. But they also could have cultivated that spiritual connection. They could have access to that same information. All they needed to do was a little more Shadow Work. I realized that even the most powerful and skilled spiritual teachers can be in their ego about how much they know.

I knew I needed to put a hard stop to what I was doing, so I stopped using the live broadcasting app. I stopped channeling with my eyes closed. I no longer claimed to be channeling certain Galactic or spiritual energies. I fell off the map of the online world and focused on my body and my process of getting to natural home birth.

I share this story with you not only to expose myself but also to help you expose other spiritual teachers who may be struggling with the same shadow. I'm a good person, And it started happening for me. I liked the feeling of people waiting with bated breath for what I would say next. If you have a spiritual teacher who you can't question or isn't willing to admit any of these traits within themselves, run.

I thought I was following my intuition. I was using my intuition to connect with these other realms. I was using my intuition to guide me to different sacred sites. To place certain crystals in those sites for activation and healing. I was using my intuition when I saw the visions and had spiritual experiences in those places. And yet, I was using my intuition from a place of ego. To feed my wounded inner child. Beware of the spiritual teacher who does this without self-awareness. And beware of doing this yourself.

Now, I keep myself in check. When I'm channeling, I do it with my eyes open, and it doesn't matter where or who the information is coming from. It doesn't even matter that I'm the one channeling it.

The message is what matters. That's the main difference between spirituality and religion. Religion focuses on the messenger, while true spirituality focuses on the message. The message is what will carry on beyond any messenger. The message is an idea that can't die. The message is the source.

I'm very aware of my own Shadow Work. I walk my talk. I continue to practice healthy boundaries. I question myself to see if what I want to share comes from my intuition or ego. The best barometer I've found to be able to do this is my body.

Remember that the body is present and has no choice but to be in the present moment. That the present moment is all there is. Your mind can fool you into thinking you're coming from your intuition when you're not. Connecting with your body is the best way to know the truth for sure. Let's dive into a super quick practice to connect with your body and check in with your yes and no.

Checking in with your Yes and No

This is an accurate way to check in with your intuition, and it's also a very easy practice to overthink. For this exercise, set the intention to get your mind out of the way. To allow your intuition and subtle senses to speak to you. Checking in with your yes and no is a great way to make a decision. To assess how you really feel about someone or decide which direction to move next.

Depending on which intuitive sense is primarily presenting for you now, your yes and no experience may be slightly different. You may get body sensations, see some things in your mind's eye, or hear some things in your mind's ear. For the purposes of this exercise, let's remove claircognizance so that you have a better chance of trusting and acting on the answer you get.

Practice

- Sit somewhere quietly. Outside would be best, but definitely sit on the floor cross-legged.

- Straighten your spine without overextending it.

- Take three deep breaths in through your nose and out through your mouth.

- Place your left hand on your heart and your right hand on your solar plexus, right above your belly button.

- First, ask yourself a very obvious yes question and a very obvious no question. This could be as simple as asking, is my name _____?

When you say your name correctly, notice what you sense.

Do you feel a relaxation or opening in your body? Do you see something in your mind's eye? Do you hear a song or a sound inside your head? Pause and notice. You can check your yes a few times.

- Before checking your no, take three more deep breaths through your nose and out through your mouth.

When you say your name incorrectly, notice what you sense.

Do you feel a tightness or tension in your body? Do you see something different in your mind's eye? Do you hear a different song or sound inside your head? Pause and notice. You can check your no a few times.

Once you have an understanding of your yes and no, you can move on to other questions. Questions related to:

- Decisions you need to make

- Relationships and people in your life

- Directions you want to move in

- Projects you may want to start

For a PDF Version of this practice that you can print out, visit ***www.ciararubin.com/yakbookresources...***

Asking for signs

Looking for signs is a great way to validate your intuition. Signs give you confirmation from the physical world around you. Most signs will come in the form of visual or audio expressions or echoes of whatever you're asking about.

If you're ever struggling with a decision, wondering whether you should do something, or reach out to someone, ask for a sign. You can do this in your head, but it's even more effective if you do it out loud.

You can say, *"Thank you, God/Universe, for giving me a sign in the physical world that I will easily recognize and immediately understand."*

You can get specific with the sign you want to see and even set a time limit.

For example, you can ask to see a yellow butterfly as a confirmation within the next 12 to 24 hours.

If you don't see your sign within that time, that's also a sign, typically a no from the universe.

If you leave the sign open in terms of what it will be, it could be anything! It could be a sequence of repeating numbers or Angel numbers. It could be a billboard you see while driving or a conversation you overhear. The sign could be a song that comes on to your playlist or that you hear playing in the space where you are.

It doesn't matter if you leave the sign open or ask for something specific. The important thing is that you set the intention to receive a sign, and then you allow yourself to receive it.

Do not start looking everywhere for your sign! That holds an energy of anxiety and will actually push your sign away. Set your intention, set a time frame if you like, and let it go. Remember, if you don't see your sign, that's also a sign!

For a PDF Version of this practice that you can print out, visit ***www.ciararubin.com/yakbookresources...***

Pendulums & Cards

Pendulums are a fun tool to get answers to a yes or no question. Like checking in with your yes or no, once you get a pendulum, you'll need to check in with the pendulum's yes and no.

Pendulums are basically weighted objects at the end of a chain or a string. They use the energetic Matrix around you to gauge the energy and frequency of your question. They use the energy of your higher self to give you an answer that's in alignment with your highest good.

Obvi, you're not allowed to influence the movement of your pendulum at all while you're holding it. You're also not allowed to overthink whether you're influencing the pendulum. Be honest with yourself, use discernment, and again allow and receive the answer.

Cards, meaning oracle cards and tarot cards, are my fave tools for validating your intuition! The excitement of pulling cards when you don't know what's on the other side. The visual beauty and pictures on the cards... It's such a fun way to guide and validate your intuition.

Tarot cards are actually the main tool I use to validate my intuition on the reg. In the next chapter, we're going to dive into intuitive tarot. Don't worry! I assure you that this is very safe and can be a very easy practice. There is no need to memorize card meanings, complex astrological correspondences, etc.

If you're interested in the scholarly side of the tarot, that's amazing! This book will teach you how to let go of some of that structure. To use your intuition to get accurate, specific messages and answers.

Chapter 20:
Intuitive Tarot

With intuitive Tarot, you'll very clearly be able to read and interpret the messages your intuition is sending you. You'll turn those messages into practical action steps.

A Lil' Story

When I first started playing around with Tarot cards, I had no idea how it would change my life. I once heard a Tarot expert say that tarot is a bridge to a different way of seeing the world and seeing yourself. I agree with that.

Using the Tarot will give you a shift in perspective that makes you see things more metaphysically. It loosens your grip on the material world while still allowing you to be part of it. Walking Between Worlds, the physical and the spiritual, is the only way you'll be able to tap into every ounce of potential that you have.

Oracle cards are fun! They're a great introduction to the art and divination practice of reading cards. The Tarot, however, has an energy all its own. No one knows where it came from; it's highly debated. The system or framework of the Tarot makes it superior to oracle cards, when it comes to getting specific answers to make your next steps clear and obvious.

At first, I was doing readings for myself and took a card-reading course. Then, after accidentally coming out of the spiritual closet on Facebook, I started doing readings for other people. The validation that comes with doing readings for other people is unmatched.

I highly suggest doing a little bit of this either free or paid when you're starting out. Especially if you're second-guessing and overthinking whether what you're getting is accurate. You'll be astounded, just as I was, when you get specific names, ailments, or causes of death.

Like seriously, how in the hell would I possibly know the name of your late Grandma's dog!? It popped out of my mouth more than once. It made me believe that my intuition was real, accurate, and helpful in unlocking other people's limiting beliefs.

What I'm going to teach you is how to see yourself in the cards. But first, we need to get real about some things.

Real Quick (Tarot isn't evil or hard)

Tarot cards are little pieces of cardstock with little pictures on them. Sometimes, the imagery can be a little dark. But when you remember that the tarot is a reflection of the entire human experience, you have to accept that some parts of your life are or have been dark.

Tarot cards are simply another way to get to know yourself. If some schools of thought deem that evil, it's time to let go of those archaic fear and control-based beliefs.

And let's get this out of the way: tarot is not hard. Yes, it has complexity. You can add whatever level of complexity you'd like. You can also completely simplify it like I'm going to do here. There's no wrong way to read the tarot, so don't let the old-world, new-age tarot snobs tell you any differently.

You don't have to be a third generation wicca, you don't have to wait for someone else to gift you a deck, and you don't have to have any "special powers" (although throughout the process of this book, you've been developing your intuitive powers!). The tarot is for everyone and anyone who wants to walk between worlds and see themselves in a new, more true kind of way.

Tarot, In a Nutshell

The tarot deck has two parts: the major Arcana and the minor arcana.

Major Arcana are 22 cards numbered 0 to 21. These cards cover the major life experiences or major turning points in your life.

The minor Arcana has four suits, like regular playing cards, and those suits are:

- Wands
- Cups
- Swords
- Pentacles

Each suit is numbered Ace through 10, and there are also four court cards in each suit:

- The Page
- The Knight
- The Queen
- The King

The minor Arcana covers the more day-to-day Life Experiences.

If you'd like a little tarot card meaning cheat sheet, check out the one I made for you at the back of this book. It'll give you little catchphrase meanings for each card. You don't need any of that info to give yourself or someone else an accurate message/answer, but it's fun to have!

Which Deck, tho?!

One of the most overwhelming parts of reading tarot is deciding which deck you'll get. There are two main traditional Decks that most other tarot decks are based on:

- The Rider Waite Smith Tarot
- The Thoth Tarot.

There are thousands of tarot decks out there, all with different aesthetics and energy.

Some decks have different interpretations of the names of the Major Arcana cards. Some decks have different interpretations of the minor arcana suits. Some decks call each of the court cards a bit differently. But they're all based on the same system.

When you're first starting out, I'd recommend getting cards that have some of the meanings written on them. It gives you a good jumping-off point.

The biggest recommendation I can give you is to get a deck that you think is pretty. Get a deck you love and feel excited to play around with. Because if you don't wanna play with your deck, you won't use it; if you don't use it, it won't help you.

Get two or three decks and see which one you connect with the best! Now that we've got a lot of the practical stuff out of the way, let's dive into the actual process of intuitive tarot.

Everything is Part of the Reading

The thing you need to know about intuitive tarot is that everything is part of the reading. I mean, EVERYTHING. Wherever you are, you'll have certain sights around you, things you hear, and things you feel.

If you hear a bird chirping outside, that's part of the reading.

If you see an insect crawling near you, that's part of the reading.

If your kids are screaming in the background, that's part of the reading.

If you get a sensation in your body, that is part of the reading!

I want you to get used to opening your intuitive senses while playing with your tarot cards. Lean on your primary intuitive sense while shuffling and pulling your cards.

I Want You To Word Vomit

This comes into play more when you're doing a reading for someone else, but it could for you as well. I would recommend doing a reading for yourself out loud. It gets the information out of your head. Then, you can distill what your intuition is giving you into a verbal message.

You could even record yourself on your phone speaking it out loud. This puts you on the spot in a way that makes the reading more powerful, impactful, and accurate. You're less likely to get in your own way and think yourself out of an intuitive hit.

But yes, I literally want you to word vomit! Say the first thing that pops into your head. I know you've been conditioned to stop yourself from saying the first thing that pops into your head. While that's a very useful and tactful social skill, it'll trip you up when it comes to the tarot. So let it out, girl!

The Intuitive Reading "What, What, What?!"

These are the general guidelines to follow when doing an intuitive tarot reading.

1. What's happening in the picture?

Like, literally, what do you see? What are the figures, animals, objects, symbols, colors?

2. What are you immediately drawn to?

After assessing the entire card, cover and uncover it with your hand and see it with fresh eyes. Which part of the card are your eyes immediately drawn to?

3. What associations do you have with it?

What comes up for you in relation to the part of the card you're drawn to? If it's a person or figure, what does it make you feel? Who does it remind you of? If it's a color, what does that color make you think of? This could be:

- A song or a vision that pops into your head
- A feeling
- A pop culture reference
- It could remind you of something in your life.

Follow the trail of your association. Explore how it could relate to the challenges and elements you're currently facing.

Try it!

Write your responses in your journal or workbook.

Ask in your head or out loud, "What do I need to know right now?"

Pull one card.

Apply the Intuitive Reading What, what, whats:

1. ***What's happening in the picture?***

2. ***What are you immediately drawn to?***

3. ***What associations do you have with this?***

Chapter 21:
The Actual Reading

A lot of my clients and students get tripped up on how to do the actual reading. First of all, I want to tell you there is no right or wrong way to do a reading. There is no right or wrong way to shuffle the cards. But I'm happy to give you a little bit of direction.

In any reading, be sure to apply the Intuitive Reading *What, What, Whats!*

- Shuffle your cards how you like. You can do a poker shuffle, a sloppy shuffle, it doesn't matter.

- Allow three cards to stick out of the deck as you shuffle.

- Place each card face down in front of you, left to right.

Here are two three-card spreads you can choose from:

The Simple AF Spread

This is my go-to spread! It's great for any question. Especially when you're wanting to know what action you should take. Or for my favorite question: "What do I need to know right now?"

Card 1: The Basis of the Situation

This card will tell you exactly what's happening at the moment. Or will tell you exactly what's causing the situation you're asking about. Your interpretation of this card will provide the basis for the rest of the reading.

Card 2: What You Need to Know

This card will tell you what you need to be aware of. It may clear something unclear. Or it'll help you cultivate self-awareness in how you are contributing to or co-creating the situation you're asking about.

Card 3: Practical Action Step

This card will tell you what you need to do or what energy you need to embody to make the situation successful and have a positive outcome. It also may give you a warning of what not to do.

Okay, now try it!

Question:

Card 1

Card 2

Card 3

Conclusion:

The Past, Present, and Potential Future

This spread helps you see the potential energy of what may be manifesting in the near future. Or you can look at a longer time span as well.

The most important word in this spread is potential. There is no such thing as "future telling." The future changes in every moment based on your:

- Beliefs
- Thoughts
- Feelings
- Actions.

The best you can do is look at the potential energy. You can change your course if it's moving toward something you don't like. Sometimes, challenges and dark periods are unavoidable. They're often the path of least resistance to the most amount of learning, self-awareness, and personal growth.

The tarot will always give you advice from your higher self. Sometimes, this does lead you into challenging things that teach you big lessons. Ones that take you to your next level of success much faster.

Card 1: The Past

This card will cover the themes and things you've been going through in the recent past.

Card 2: The Present

This card will cover the themes and things you are currently facing.

Card 3: The Potential Future

This card will show you an energetic snapshot of what'll happen if you continue on the same path you're currently on. If it looks good, don't change anything. If it looks like something you'd rather not experience, take a look at what beliefs, habits, or thoughts may be leading you in that direction. Course correct with a little Shadow Work.

Okay, now try it!

Question:

Card 1

Card 2

Card 3

Conclusion:

Using Your Intuitive Senses

I will teach you how to use your intuitive senses to get messages from the environment around you. You could be pulling cards while utilizing these skills or not. Using the cards as a baseline or jumping-off point is good for the intuitive hits you're already getting.

What Comes In Lightning Fast?

When you're pulling cards, there'll be a download of information that comes in before you turn the cards over.

Record a voice note on your phone and speak it out loud. That way, you don't get in your head wondering if it's really coming from your higher self or not. This download is your Claircognizance at work!

Check In With Your Body

As you begin shuffling the cards, take a deep breath and tune in to your body. What sensations do you notice? Where do you have tension in your body?

Tension is always a clue; it will lead you to unlock a limiting belief or an answer to what could be holding you back from your next step. You can relate the sensations or tension you notice to a particular chakra. Or you can relate it to how you're feeling.

For example, if your stomach gurgles, it could be related to your sense of self-confidence. If you find yourself clearing your throat or coughing, you may need to speak your truth or set a boundary that may feel uncomfortable.

If you notice that your hands and feet are cold, it could mean you have cold feet about something. Remember that your body is present and has an ancient intelligence of its own. You can always trust the messages you get from your body.

What Do You See?

This is as simple as it seems. What do you see around you in your immediate environment? You can even use the "Intuitive Reading What What What" written above. What's happening around you? What are you immediately drawn to, and what are your associations with it? It could be:

- An object
- A person
- An insect or animal
- A photograph

Whatever you see will somehow relate to your situation or the question you're asking.

What Do You Hear?

In the moment you're shuffling and pulling your cards, what do you hear around you? You may say nothing, but I assure you we never live in a silent world. You may hear:

- The sounds of nature out your window
- The sound of your air conditioner or your refrigerator
- The sounds of people inside or outside the room
- Music.

What do you hear, and what are your associations with those sounds?

Try it

Write your responses in your journal or workbook.

Shuffle your cards while asking, "What do I need to know right now?"

Keep your senses open as you shuffle.

Pull one card.

What pops into your head?

What do you feel in your body?

What do you see around you?

What do you hear?

How can you use the input you're getting and apply it to your question?

How can you use the input you're getting to what you see on the card?

How can you apply the input and the card to what's going on in your life right now?

Remember Who's Psychic

You're the one who's psychic and intuitive, not the cards. The cards are beautiful, mystical objects that carry the energy of the creator of the deck. They also carry your energy once you buy and begin playing with the deck.

Always remember that you have the answers within you, you always know, and that your cards will never lie to you. You are psychic. Your intuitive senses will play a starring role in helping you create the life you've always dreamed of. The life you're meant to live.

Chapter 22:
Remember Who You Are

Remember who you are. This was the phrase that kept repeating in my head over and over again. Through the years, I awakened to my psychic abilities. I chose myself and went on a self-discovery adventure that saved my marriage. As I walked through the temples of Egypt, I felt like I was returning home.

Remember who you are. This phrase is deeply ingrained in me, and I imagine it could also be in you. It means the beginning of a deep journey into recalling all the parts of yourself you banished as a child. It's a journey of discovering your multidimensionality. To recalling all the lives you've lived on this planet and beyond.

Remembering who you are is about remembering your strength as a sovereign being. It's about remembering that you are one with everyone and everything in this Universe.

This is the path of intuition development. It is a constant, lifelong process of remembering who you are. Clearing out the shadow so you can experience more of who you are. Taking proper care of all that you are. Receiving the exquisite validation that your physical world is surrounded and led by a spiritual one.

You are a powerful spiritual being with many abilities right at your fingertips. Your intuition is just the beginning. My hope for you is that you commit this process that you've learned in this book to your cellular memory, deep into your bones. And that forever more, as you walk through this life, you remember that you can walk between worlds. That it's not only safe to do so, it's your calling.

You have the potential to become a full-fledged light worker. A spiritual coach, spiritual teacher, or practitioner. You can use your intuition to help others in a way that will help them remember who they are.

We need more lightworkers. We're in a precarious time on our planet when the darkness within us is rearing its ugly head. There's so much suffering and so much chaos. We need more people who can be still in the eye of that storm.

Remembering who you are is also about becoming a soldier who does not fight. You are a soldier who recognizes that the only person you have the power to change is yourself. As you change yourself and awaken again and again, you're no longer subject to the whims of a fear-based society. This is true power, true sovereignty.

Many people avoid it because they would rather have an easy, instantly gratifying solution, like "activism" or shouting at power structures that be (WERE!). Yes, your anger is sacred. Yes, some are here to tear down the structures that are not in alignment with an awakened humanity.

And also, these systems will collapse on themselves if we stop paying close attention. Commit to paying attention to what's going on within you. Allow your sacred anger to burn away all the parts of you that do not believe in your power and in your absolute love.

Remember who you are and that the only way out is in and through. Awakening one person at a time is definitely a long game. But it's the only way to overcome the cycles of civilization creation and destruction.

As I answer my calling, I'll create ripple effects that help others to choose awakening. As you answer your calling, you'll create an even bigger ripple effect.

You might resonate with the concept of ascension. It's true that we are in an Ascension cycle on the progression of the Equinox. And so, in truth, we've already made it to 5th dimensional consciousness.

I feel it deep inside my soul. No matter how dark, how chaotic it gets here on this planet and within our Matrix-created structures. Somehow, we will still rebirth ourselves at our next level of potential.

You are part of this rebirth process, a crucial part. Your choice to awaken and develop your intuition is nothing short of a miracle. Remember who you are, and share that remembering with everyone who will listen.

You're called to a higher level of service. You're called to be all you can be, to illustrate to yourself and others what is possible to achieve in this life. It's been an absolute honor to connect with you in this way. I love you today and every day.

Works Cited

l Aron, Elaine N. PHD. 2023. The Highly Sensitive Person. Retrieved November 13, 2023 from hsperson.com

l Evans, Kenya. April 18, 2022. Witnessing Violence on TV: What the Oscars Can Tell Us About Trauma. Retrieved November 13, 2023 from skywaybehavioralhealth.com

l Gunnars, Kris BSc. December 4, 2019. How to Identify and Manage Food Addiction. Retrieved November 13, 2023 from healthline.com

l Nall, Rachel MSN. Wilson, Debra Rose PHD. May 26, 2020. Decalcifying Your Pineal Gland: Does It Work? Retrieved November 13, 2023 from healthline.com

About the Author

In 2015, an aura reader told Ciara she was meant to be a spiritual teacher and leader. She thought the lady was crazy, but trusted a tiny gut feeling to look into it. Since then, Ciara has helped thousands of people with her intuitive work, often getting the high praise of, "how did you know that?!"

After realizing that EVERYONE has the ability to develop their intuitive and psychic abilities, Ciara started a business to spread the message. As an empath with powerful clairvoyance and clairaudience, Ciara leans on her intuition to guide all decisions in her life. This led her on a pilgrimage to Egypt, a cross country adventure that saved her marriage, and the empowered home-births of her two sons.

www.ciararubin.com
TikTok & Instagram: **@ciara.rubin**
YouTube: **Ciara Rubin**

Acknowledgments

Zach Rubin, Krissy Chin, Claire vanBemmelen, Abby Byrd,
Jessica Anderson, Masha Loddy, Taylor Barraclough,
Hay House Writer's Community, and all the other
amazing women who helped me along the way!

Heal & Activate Your Clairs

Heal & Activate Your Clairsentience

Chakra(s)	Solar Plexus & Heart
Chakra Color(s)	Yellow & Green
Chakra Diagram	

Physical Organs Associated	Solar Plexus Chakra: • Stomach • Intestines • Liver • Pancreas • Gallbladder • Diaphragm • Kidneys Heart Chakra: • Heart • Lungs • Thymus • Arms • Hands • Fingers
Physical Issues	Solar Plexus Chakra • IBS • Bloating, gas • Food sensitivities or allergies • Leaky Gut • Candida (yeast overgrowth) • Hyper or Hypoglycemia • Ulcers in the digestive system • Liver dysfunction • Spleen dysfunction • Pancreas or Gallbladder dysfunction • Diabetes Heart Chakra • Heart issues • Heart attacks • Bronchitis • Asthma • Allergies • Breast issues (lumps, cancer) • Shoulder issues • Arm or hand issues • Carpal tunnel syndrome • Poor posture

Energetic Issues	Solar Plexus Chakra • Low self-esteem or self-worth • Lack of self-confidence • Indecisiveness • Poor sense of self • People pleasing • Unexpressed anger • Resentment (of yourself or others) • Jealousy (in any relationship or situation) • Self-shame • Self-loathing • Guilt • Comparison to others (in a way that disempowers you) Heart Chakra • Emotional abuse, neglect, abandonment, or aggression • Heartbreak (partner, family member, friend) • Self-betrayal or betrayal by others • Being ignored • Feeling like no one truly loves or understands you • Needing constant reassurance or external emotional validation • Codependency • Difficulty trusting others • Inability to fully fall in love with a partner • Challenges allowing yourself to be loved • Difficulty forgiving others who've wronged you • Difficulty forgiving yourself • Ghosting people

How to Heal	**Heal Your Solar Plexus Chakra**
	Some tips to heal your solar plexus chakra:
	• Tap into and fire up your free will.
	• Figure out and commit to a diet that reflects your ideal lifestyle and what works best for your body.
	• Meditation
	• Exercise (that you enjoy! It doesn't have to be intense cardio)
	• Develop a nightly bedtime routine that helps you wind down at least 1-2 hours before you want to be asleep.
	• Mirror work and affirmations (married with Shadow Work)
	• OWN YOUR POWER
	• Channel your anger into something creative and productive
	• Setting healthy boundaries and doing what's best for you
	• Develop a healthy self-care routine
	• Heal how you feel about any relationships with men in your life. The ones who let you down, hurt you, or aren't fulfilling their potential and modeling that for you.
	• Color Therapy
	• Wear or keep the color yellow around you.
	• Create art with the color yellow.
	Heal Your Heart Chakra
	Some tips to heal your heart chakra:
	• Meditation (focused on your heart)
	• Journaling
	• Expressing your love to loved ones, family members, friends, and pets.
	• Allow yourself to receive love from others.
	• Receive compliments with grace.
	• Do things that you love, just for fun!
	• Set the intention to journey toward unconditional love and self-love.
	• Choose to see that everything serves your highest good, even if it doesn't make logical sense.
	• Self-forgiveness
	• Self-compassion
	• Develop self-appreciation and self-loving practices and habits.
	• Mirror Work
	• Forgive others
	• Heal how you feel about any relationships with women in your life. The ones who let you down, hurt you, or aren't fulfilling their potential and modeling that for you.
	• Color Therapy
	• Wear or keep the color green around you.
	• Create art with the color green.

Heal & Activate Your Clairvoyance

Chakra	Third Eye
Chakra Color	Indigo
Chakra Diagram	
Physical Organs Associated	• Eyes • Brain • Pineal gland

Physical Issues	• Glaucoma
	• Cataracts
	• Blindness, any level
	• Needing glasses, contact lenses
	• Migraines
	• Headaches
	• Strokes
	• Seizures
	• Mental disturbance or illness
	  • Bipolar disorder
	  • Schizophrenia
	  • Depression
	  • Anxiety
	• Brain Tumors

Energetic Issues	• Resistance to new ideas • Resistance to change • Feeling that your beliefs are the only "correct" beliefs • Closed minded-ness • Lack of self-awareness • Trouble remembering your dreams • Turning a "blind eye" to others • Enabling others' addictions or negative behavior patterns • Struggling to be creative or use your imagination

How to Heal	**Heal Your Third Eye Chakra**
	Some tips to heal your third eye chakra:
	• Honor your need for solitude
	• Keep your spaces clean and organized
	• Meditation
	• Dream Journaling
	• Color Therapy
	   • Wear or surround yourself with indigo blue.
	   • Create art with the color indigo blue.

Heal & Activate Your Clairaudience

Chakra	Throat Chakra
Chakra Color	Light Blue
Chakra Diagram	
Physical Organs Associated	• Throat • Neck • Shoulders • Mouth • Tongue • Teeth • Gums • Chin • Jaw • Sinuses • Vocal Chords • Esophagus • Ears • Thyroid

Physical Issues	• Chronic bad breath or halitosis • TMJ • Tightness in the jaw or lockjaw • Grinding the teeth • Chronic sinus issues or allergies • Tonsillitis • Chronic strep or sore throat • Stiff or sore neck or shoulders • Neck or upper spinal issues or injuries • Tooth decay • Chronic cavities • Root canals • Thyroid issues • Losing your voice (laryngitis, hoarseness)

Energetic Issues	• Lying of any kind
	  • Lying to protect yourself or someone else
	  • Lying by omission
	  • White lies
	  • Anytime you're lying to yourself
	• Being hushed or shamed for being talkative or loud
	• Stifling of your creativity or creative impulse
	• Fearing rejection for being yourself
	• Not speaking your truth, not speaking up for what you want or believe
	• Demanding what you want (from ego)
	• Biting your tongue
	• Swallowing your words
	• Putting your foot in your mouth
	• Being passive aggressive

How to Heal	**Heal Your Throat Chakra**
	Some tips to heal your throat chakra:
	• Journaling
	• Chanting or Singing Meditation
	• Living, communicating, and acting within your highest truth
	• Express yourself creatively
	• Express yourself honestly in healthy ways
	• Color therapy
	  • Wear or surround yourself with light blue.
	  • Create art with the color light blue.

Heal & Activate Your Claircognizance

Chakra	Crown Chakra
Chakra Color	Violet
Chakra Diagram	
Physical Organs Associated	• Brain • Pineal gland • Pituitary gland • Hypothalamus • Central nervous system

Physical Issues	• Anxiety • Fears within your mind • Bipolar • Depression • Insomnia • ADHD • Headaches • Strokes • Brain Tumors • Epilepsy • Parkinson's • Alzheimer's • Dementia

Energetic Issues	• Trauma-informed belief systems
	• Fear
	• Breaking of trust or mistrust
	  • This can manifest as others betraying you and is usually a reflection of how you feel about God, Spirit, and yourself.
	• Feeling disconnected from God, Source energy, the Universe, and/or your spirituality
	• Thinking that your beliefs are the only "right ones"
	  • Do you hold too tightly to your beliefs, or do you allow them to change as you learn and grow?
	• Do you believe you are connected to and live in a supportive Universe?

How to Heal	**Heal Your Crown Chakra**
	Some tips to heal your crown chakra:
	• Examine your beliefs and belief systems on the reg.
	• What beliefs might be holding you back?
	• Where did those beliefs come from?
	• Cultivate mindfulness
	  • Self-awareness
	  • Gratitude
	• Release attachment to specific outcomes
	• Surrendering to divine will and divine timing.
	• Release your need to control others.
	• Meditation (obvi!)
	• Color Therapy
	  • Wear or surround yourself with purple.
	  • Create art with the color purple.

The 7 Steps of Shadow Work

Step 1: Awareness	If you're going to heal a shadow, the first step is to become aware of what that shadow even is. This is going to be a surface-level problem or challenge. Use this process to become aware of the negative behavior trait(s) you want to change about yourself or the area of your life you want to improve. Here are some examples of places to look for shadows: • A relationship that ended (romantic, friendship) • A difficult family relationship • Friendship(s) that feel unfulfilling or draining • Challenges with your child • Challenges with your partner • Traumatic experiences, which can be from childhood on, ranging from: • Full-on physical, mental, or emotional trauma • Low-key embarrassment or small infractions over years • Parts of your job that you hate • People at work that annoy you • Neighbors who annoy you • Parts of your business that aren't working (or aren't working as well as they should) • Any aspect of your life that you regularly struggle with or complain about • Any aspect of your life that you historically struggle with or complain about

Practice:
Pick one thing from your own life that you want to heal, and write your responses in your journal or workbook.

AWARENESS: What Shadow do you want to heal? Pick the first thing that comes to mind: the low-hanging fruit. Make a list of all the Shadows that come to the forefront of your mind.

Write the answer to this question: How does awareness of this/these shadow(s) make you feel?

Step 2: Intention	Now that you're aware of the shadow, it's time to set your intention. Intentions are a powerful and crucial part of any spiritual and emotional work. Your intentions (whether you're aware of them or not) are paving the way for all manifestations and the reality you experience.

Practice:
INTENTION: So, what do you want? How do you want to feel after healing this shadow? What do you hope shifts in your life as a result of facing this demon? Write your responses in your journal or workbook.

Step 3: The Root	Awareness and intention will pave the way to finding the root of your issue. Awareness was about the surface problem, the effect of your shadow.
	The cause of the shadow will be different. It's linked to a limiting belief, dysfunctional behavior, and/or traumatic situation.
	The limiting beliefs that live in your subconscious are not always immediately obvious. If discovering the root of your shadow takes a few days or even a few weeks, I don't want you to lose heart or give up!
	Finding the root takes a little exploration. I'll make it easy by applying the triggers exercise.

Practice:

THE ROOT: Use the shadow you're choosing for this exercise to embark on a similar exploration. Discover the root trauma and/or limiting beliefs connected to it. Write your answers in your journal or workbook.

The Shadow (copy this from your Awareness step):

Trigger Exercise:

What triggered or hurt you most about this?

What unhealthy behaviors (of theirs) are you seeing within these triggers?

Do you do any of those things, or have you in the past? Yep.

Why do you do those things?

The Root(s):

| Step 4: Feel It | Now, you've gotten down to the heart of the matter. It's time to let yourself feel all the feelings.

This is something that most people avoid. It's safe to get used to allowing yourself to feel these feelings.

These feelings could include:
• Confusion
• Anxiety
• Anger
• Disgust
• Frustration
• Terror
• Hatred
• Loathing
• Sadness
• Deep sadness
• Depression

True strength is the ability to feel deeply. To give yourself the space and time to feel all your emotions so that they move through you and don't keep you stuck. |

The 4 Physical Release Types
Though the energy stuck inside of you is mental or emotional, you're still a physical being. So, to dissolve your shadow, you must experience that release physically. What follows are four techniques you can use by themselves and altogether to "feel it" while facing any shadow.

1. Journaling

Writing down your feelings is a sure-fire way to bring those feelings back into your conscious awareness. Typing it out on the computer or into a note on your phone just doesn't have the same flavor as pen to paper.

I invite you to set a timer for 10 minutes and allow your pen to flow. Even if you're unsure what to write, write that you're not sure what to write, and keep going! I'll give you a prompt at the end of this chapter so that you can explore the shadow you're working on through writing.

2. Speaking

Saying your feelings out loud is powerful. Sometimes, it can be difficult to say the things you want to say to someone who hurt you in the moment. And so those feelings and words stay stuck in your throat and energy field.

Try doing the writing exercise first, and then read your writing out loud to yourself. This is especially helpful if the writing alone didn't make you cry.

Music is a powerful form of artistic expression that is full of emotion. It can help you get in touch with your deeper, shadowy emotions.

All you have to do is reflect on a song that makes you feel the way the shadow you're facing makes you feel.

You don't have to be a singer for this to work. In fact, YOUR voice singing along to a song that makes you feel something is the most effective tool. Rather than listening to someone else sing. So:

- Find your song
- Play it in a place where you can be alone for about 10 to 15 minutes
- Sing along with it while reflecting on the feelings brought up by the shadow you're facing.
- Allow all feelings to come to the surface with patience and compassion for yourself.

3. Sweating

Releasing stuck feelings through sweat is totally a thing. We know by now that water holds emotion. There are a few different ways you can do this. You can set the intention to release your feelings before you go into a sauna. Or before an exercise session. You can imagine the feelings and limiting beliefs pouring off of you through your sweat.

4. Crying

All the other physical release types can, and SHOULD, lead to this one: crying. Crying is the fastest and most permanent way to release shadow and limiting beliefs. It ensures that you feel any lingering negative emotions. That you're truly healing from any trauma you've experienced.

When you cry, your body literally vibrates. On an energetic level, your body is moving stuck energy up and out of your aura and being.

If you have trouble getting to a place where you can cry during your Shadow Work process, use the above physical release types first.

- Journaling your feelings is a good way to start to get back in touch with those forbidden feelings.
- Then, you can read your writing aloud. Or simply speak aloud the things you've always wanted to say.
- Then, you can play a song you feel relates to how you feel about the situation and sing along.
- You could even go for a run or walk while reflecting on the situation. The movement of your body could allow the tears to come.

Crying is crucial to letting go of your traumas in a way that stops them from continuing to manifest. Even if they do, you're no longer beholden to or triggered by those things because you've truly let them go. Once you allow yourself to cry, your shadow no longer has power over you.

Practice:

In your journal, free write about the Shadow you're currently facing. Write at the top of the page: "What do I need to remember and feel about (insert your situation/trauma/behavior/root?)."

Then, set a timer for 10 minutes and write non-stop. If you're not sure what to write, write "I'm not sure what to write," and keep going until the timer stops. Let it all out in the confidence that no one else will ever see this (you can even burn it afterward to make sure). Don't try to be proper or polite. Dig deep.

Now, read your writing aloud. If there are any emotions or tears that come up, stop reading for a moment. Allow yourself to cry until you feel the crying come to a stopping point. Then, continue until you've read the entire piece.

If you still haven't cried, or if you feel there's more emotion, reflect on a song that relates to what you're facing. Go with the first song that pops into your head. Listen to the song, sing along, and allow yourself to feel the feels and cry.

Step 5: Let The Light In	Now you've done the gnarly work of feeling your feelings. You've had a catharsis. It's time for the very important step of letting the light in. When you release stuck energy, emotion, and shadow, you create a void within your energy field. The universe always fills a void. So, immediately after clearing space within your energy field, you must intend, imagine, and allow light to fill that void.

Practice:
Put on a five-minute meditation track or song that lights you up on the inside. Sit down with your eyes closed. Imagine light pouring into the space you've created with your catharsis. Extra points if you do this meditation while sitting outside in the sun. Guided meditation recorded on *www.ciararubin.com/yakbookresources.*

Step 6: Intention 2.0	Reflect on your Intention from Step 2, and adjust it now that you're seeing things more clearly. Create your new belief.

Practice:
Rewrite your intentions from Step 2 in your journal or workbook, and turn them into affirmations.
Intention:
Affirmation (New Belief):
Say your affirmations out loud to yourself 3 times. Bonus points if you put them in your phone, write them down, and put them up around your home.

Step 7: Habit Time	There are some new habits that you need to develop to make the healing permanent. To move your life in that area on an upward trajectory. For now, a simple awareness of the new habit(s) you want/need to cultivate and writing them down is important. That could also involve breaking yourself of a bad habit. Healing the shadow associated with that habit will take you far in terms of awareness. Yet, you still may find yourself in situations where the old habit is triggered. For all things habit-breaking and building, I recommend the book *Atomic Habits* by James Clear.

Practice:
Brainstorm in your journal or workbook.
Habit to break:
Habit to build:

Tarot Meanings Cheat Sheet

The Major Arcana

0 THE FOOL **Leap of Faith**	1 THE MAGICIAN **You can Manifest it.**
2 HIGH PRIESTESS **Be the psychic observer.**	3 THE EMPRESS **Creative & Abundant AF.**
4 THE EMPEROR **Structure & Leadership**	5 THE HIEROPHANT **Tradition & Teachers**
6 THE LOVERS **Choices & True love.**	7 THE CHARIOT **Success!**
8 STRENGTH **nuff said.**	9 THE HERMIT **Disconnect to reconnect.**
10 WHEEL OF FORTUNE **Shits moving forward!**	11 JUSTICE **Is gonna be yours.**
12 HANGED MAN **A pause for perspective.**	13 DEATH **Transformation.**
14 TEMPERANCE **Healing & Chill.**	15 THE DEVIL **Addictions & Ego**
16 THE TOWER **Shits blowing UP.**	17 THE STAR **What're your #goals?**
18 THE MOON **Listen to your intuition**	19 THE SUN **Yes! All good!**
20 JUDGEMENT **Awakening.**	21 THE WORLD **Culmination. Winning**

The minor arcana

Suit of Wands

ACE New inspiration	2 Envisioning the future.	3 Ships starting to come in.
4 Happy Home.	5 Conflict.	6 Victory, but there's more.
7 Rising up no matter the odds.	8 Things moving forward fast.	9 Weary & almost there!
10 Put down the burden.	PAGE Starting a New venture.	KNIGHT Message/ New Career Opportunity
QUEEN Stand in your Power	KING Use your Charisma.	

Suit of Swords

ACE Breakthrough.	2 Indecision.	3 Heartbreak. Sadness.
4 Rest. Meditate on it.	5 Victory at ALL costs.	6 Things get better.
7 Dishonesty.	8 Illusion of being stuck.	9 Overthinking. Analysis paralysis.
10 Drop the drama. Let it die.	PAGE Use your smarts.	KNIGHT In over your head. Use discernment.
QUEEN Edit that shit that no longer serves you.	KING Use your power.	

Suit of Cups

ACE New emotional experience!	2 LOVEEE	3 Celebration!
4 Lack mentality. You're missing something.	5 Crying over spilled milk.	6 Inner child innocence.
7 Lots of choices.	8 Walking away.	9 Wishes come true!
10 Ultimate emotional fulfillment.	PAGE Psychic & creative.	KNIGHT Offers of romance or love.
QUEEN Empowered Empath.	KING Emotionally available.	

Suit of Pentacles

ACE New money making opportunity.	2 Balance & intentionality.	3 Collabs!
4 Hold on to what you've got.	5 Feeling left out. Lack.	6 Receiving abundance.
7 Patience. Seeds well planted.	8 Head down & do the work.	9 Successful self-employed woman.
10 Wealth. Legacy. YASS.	PAGE Successful new endeavor.	KNIGHT Slow & steady wins the race. Opportunity you can count on.
QUEEN Grounded wealthy vibes.	KING He's got money mindset on LOCK.	

Made in the USA
Monee, IL
27 April 2025

16441447R00154